# SACR
# RHYTHMS

## *The Monastic Way Every Day*

**With an Introduction by Rt. Rev. Justin DuVall, O.S.B.**

***Edited by Br. Francis de Sales Wagner, O.S.B.***

Illustrations by Br. Martin Erspamer, O.S.B.
Cover and book design by Mary E. Bolin.
Title page photograph by Br. Matthew Mattingly, O.S.B.



ISBN 978-0-87029-466-2
Library of Congress 2011935645

Published by Abbey Press
1 Hill Drive • St. Meinrad, IN 47577
Printed by Abbey Press in the United States of America

# Contents



## Ora
(Pray)



## Labora
(Work)

## Fidelitas
### (Faithfulness)



## Conversatio
### (Conversion)

# Foreword

# Relentless Grace

*"Let the word of Christ dwell in you richly,*
*as in all wisdom you teach and admonish one another,*
*singing psalms, hymns, and spiritual songs*
*with gratitude in your hearts to God.*
*And whatever you do, in word or deed,*
*do everything in the name of the Lord Jesus,*
*giving thanks to God the father through him."*

— **Colossians 3:16-17**

St. Benedict does not refer explicitly to the above Scripture passage in his *Rule* for monks, but it succinctly expresses what the *Rule* embodies. The monastic day is designed to carry with it the word of Christ throughout its hours. In gratitude to God, we pray and we work. We do this as a community that strives to make Christ present to one another and the world in *everything* we do.

We all have our work life, family life, social life, and (if we have it at all) spiritual life. But how do these areas intersect and affect one another? The Christian life is one of unity. We worship a God who is incarnate—the Word made Flesh. All that we think, say, or do should radiate Christ.

Since monastic men and women are not immune to the temptation of living fragmented lives, the Benedictine motto *ora et labora—pray and work*—expresses the ideal of the *Rule* of St. Benedict. Lived with *faithfulness* in the context of community, it is a sacred rhythm that provides structure and direction for our daily lives and (hopefully) keeps us on the path of *conversion* and everlasting life.

These four themes and section titles for this book—*prayer, work, faithfulness, and conversion*—figure prominently in the life of monastic men and women. Our common prayer, personal prayer and growth, various works, and day-to-day living with one another are not disparate elements, but strands woven together like those of a rope to give our whole lives strength and sacred purpose. This requires commitment, humility, and the love of God.

One concrete symbol of this ideal is the corridor (or "slype," in monastic terminology) that connects our monastery and church at Saint Meinrad Archabbey in southern Indiana. Each day, after praising God in church, the monks process down the slype and directly into the monastery dining room (refectory) for our meals together. It is a reminder that whatever we do, we do for the glory of God, so that God may be glorified in all things through Jesus Christ (1 Corinthians 10:31; 1 Peter 4:11).

All this, of course, is with the recognition that the Kingdom of God is not yet fully realized. This path toward life everlasting is a journey we make *each day*. Men and women embrace the monastic way of life in response to God's call not because they are perfect, but to *become* perfect through the grace of God. Monks and nuns living according to the *Rule* of St. Benedict seek God in the ordinary, the routine, and the mundane. That is all that truly sets them apart. No matter what else they do, the ordered round of prayer in the monastery continually calls them back to listen and respond to the Word of God, who is the source of our lives.

Fr. Harry Hagan, O.S.B., our former novice-master at Saint Meinrad, likes to say that, "Monastic life is not difficult. It's relentless." The same can be said of any Christian state of life. It takes commitment, focus, and discipline to faithfully live as a Christian, whether you're a monk or not. It always has.

For those of us in the monastery, *ora et labora* is intended to be a symbiotic relationship, a rhythm of life in which intervals of communal and personal prayer, work, and our common lives together as monastic men and women are interwoven into one continuous thread. Through faithfulness, we bring our lives to prayer, and our prayer to our lives for the purpose of conversion of heart. With God's Word permeating our lives, we are confronted with ourselves and extended beyond them into the life of the church and world.

Relentless, yes. And also relentlessly full of grace.

However, as Archabbot Justin DuVall, O.S.B., points out in his introduction to this book, it is not absolutely necessary to join a monastery (though it may be for some!), for one to live this relentless grace. As Christians, we all can—indeed, *must*—embrace rhythmic lives of prayer, work, faithfulness, and conversion. "The search for God does not necessarily mean living an extraordinary life; it does mean living an ordinary life in an extraordinary way," writes Archabbot DuVall. "The practices of monastic life are not so different from the everyday tasks of ordinary people. Those who find a kindred spirit in St. Benedict through his *Rule* strive to share his mind on God, the world, and themselves."

Indeed, many Christians today yearn for a simpler, sacred, and intentional way of life that connects the everyday to the eternal. In recent years, people from many walks of life and faith traditions have increasingly turned to Benedict's *Rule* for inspiration and guidance. There also is an increasing interest in such ancient monastic practices as *lectio divina,* and the praying of the Divine Office (daily liturgical prayer based on the chanting of the Psalms), as well as the monastic way of life in general.

Monastery guesthouses and retreat centers are bursting with visitors, and many lay people are attaching themselves to a particular monastery as oblates or associates, observing the *Rule* within their own life circumstances. Books based on Benedictine spirituality have become increasingly popular in the last 20 years. People are rediscovering St. Benedict's wise, universal approach—one that is mindful, practical, and rich in human warmth, hospitality, and community.

Why is this? After all, the *Rule* of St. Benedict was written more than 1,500 years ago! One explanation worth consideration is offered by laywoman Lonni Collins Pratt and Benedictine monk Daniel Homan, co-authors of *Benedict's Way: An Ancient Monk's Insights for a Balanced Life* (2000):

> Benedict's time had much in common with our own. Life was a battle to make sense of all that was happening, a war for

> personal meaning and significant values. We aren't the first generation fighting this battle. Those who have gone before us just might have something to say that will be helpful to us, something relevant, timely, profound. We have found that Benedict is all of that.

In short, ancient wisdom is in. The Benedictine way of life has modern relevance, and offers the relentless grace—the sacred rhythms—that spiritual seekers today are looking for amid their everyday lives. Not everyone is called to be a monk or a nun, but all are called to faithfully live the Gospel, and the *Rule* of St. Benedict offers a time-honored way for *anyone* to do just that. St. Benedict's ancient words of wisdom have guided millions of people worldwide in establishing and maintaining sacred rhythms of prayer, work, faithfulness, and conversion within the context of their own lives.

With this in mind, Abbey Press' Path of Life Publications, a work of Saint Meinrad Archabbey, in 2009 began publishing a series of 12-page, four-color booklets titled *Notes from a Monastery: The Sacred Way Every Day*. Each booklet in the series focuses on a different aspect of the monastic way of life in the Benedictine tradition to assist ordinary people committed to seeking God in their everyday lives. Beautifully illustrated by Br. Martin Erspamer, O.S.B., a monk of Saint Meinrad, and skillfully designed by Mary Bolin of the Abbey Press, the booklets showcase the knowledge of religious and lay authors familiar with the Benedictine way of life.

The booklets have been very well received, and are sold in retreat centers, gift shops, and bookstores across the country. Oblates and prayer groups have also found them helpful.

*Sacred Rhythms: The Monastic Way Every Day* is a compilation of 15 of the 22 titles published thus far in the series. In addition, this book features two previously unpublished additions—an introduction with Archabbot DuVall's thoughts on the rhythms of life within Benedict's vision; and a chapter by Fr. Harry examining the principal virtues—particularly discretion—in the monastic tradition.

The book is divided into sections highlighting the broad themes outlined above—prayer, work, faithfulness, and conversion—with four chapters each focusing on more specific topics within those realms.

This entire endeavor—the booklet series, and now this companion book—has been a personal labor of love. It has been intricately woven into my own experience of prayer, work, faithfulness, and conversion since coming to Saint Meinrad Archabbey. The seeds were planted in 2007 as a novice, when Fr. Harry, my novice master, suggested I might try writing a pamphlet based on the *Rule* for our retreatants and guests. While that particular project never got off the ground, I kept it in the back of my mind. A year later, I was encouraged by Archabbot DuVall—during a somewhat difficult period in my formation as a junior monk—to flesh out the idea in the course of my newly assigned work as a writer and editor for Abbey Press Publications.

With their inspiration and encouragement, and with the assistance of my colleagues at the Abbey Press, *Notes from a Monastery* gradually took shape. Of essential importance, obviously, has been the support and contributions of my brothers in the monastery, monastic men and women from around the country (and in a few cases, beyond it), oblates, and laypersons devoted to living the sacred rhythms of the *Rule*. I am sincerely grateful to all.

These reflections do not pretend to provide answers for those seeking God within the monastic tradition, but rather to offer direction along the Christian path of life, demonstrating God's relentless grace through the sacred rhythms of prayer, work, faithfulness, and conversion. My prayer, through the intercession of St. Benedict, is that *Sacred Rhythms: The Monastic Way Every Day* will help you listen for the voice of the Lord and progress in this way of life and in faith, so that we may all prefer nothing to Christ, who brings us all together to everlasting life.

**Br. Francis de Sales Wagner, O.S.B.**
*Saint Meinrad Archabbey, July 16, 2011*
*Solemnity of Our Lady of Einsiedeln*
*Titular Feast of Archabbey Church*

Introduction

# St. Benedict's Vision: Rhythms of Life

Despite a decline in church attendance among Americans in the last 10 to 15 years, numerous surveys have disclosed a growing trend: SBNR—*spiritual but not religious.* While not affiliated with any particular denomination, people continue to describe themselves as spiritual. They perceive the doctrines and practices associated with a particular denomination as a hindrance, rather than a help, for their well-being. Although they are reluctant to accept the ways by which traditional religion embodies belief, and instead see in them limitations rather than aids, they nevertheless believe in a divine being. Consequently, they describe themselves as spiritual but not religious.

This distinction would have baffled St. Benedict. His *Rule* reflects his mind, and in that mind *religious* practices give expression to *spiritual* desires. A spirituality unmoored from a community rooted in a tradition shaped by those practices would have been inconceivable for him. He prescribed particular practices for the life of his monastery because he believed that the search for God engaged the whole person—body, mind, spirit—and the human person comes to conversion without division and in communion with others. This integration of practice and attitude finds expression in his admonition about prayer: "Let us consider, then, how we ought to behave in the presence of God and his angels, and let us stand to sing the psalms in such a way that our minds are in harmony with our voices" (Chapter 19:6-7).

In addition, St. Benedict saw no opposition between God and nature, and so the world is sacramental, mediating the God who created it. More specifically, the world is not merely nature—a self-contained system of cosmic forces that occasionally clash and at other times harmonize—as our modern thought sometimes sees it. Rather, the world came about through the act of creation and is sustained by the loving providence of God whose will brought it into being and draws it to the perfection of his Kingdom. If things are less than perfect, it is because human sinfulness has wounded not just our nature but creation itself. The whole of monastic life thrives on the desire to return to God "from whom [we] have drifted through the sloth of disobedience" (Prologue 2). Monks make this return in concert with the whole of creation to which they themselves belong.

St. Benedict, therefore, sees the world with a kind of double vision, one eye looking at the beauty of God's handiwork, the other at the chaos of sin still to be overcome by God's providence. The Orthodox theologian David Bentley Hart beautifully describes this way of looking at the world in *The Doors of the Sea*:

> ... the Christian should see two realities at once, one world (as it were) within another: one the world as we all know it, in all its beauty and terror, grandeur and dreariness, delight and anguish; and the other the world in its first and ultimate truth, not simply "nature" but "creation," an endless sea of glory, radiant with the beauty of God in every part, innocent of all violence. To see in this way is to rejoice and mourn at once, to regard the world as a mirror of infinite beauty, but as glimpsed through the veil of death; it is to see creation in chains, but beautiful as in the beginning of days.

The integration of these two ways of looking at the world gives St. Benedict's understanding of the return to God a firm purpose and a defined path. The path is marked by particular practices and pursued with spiritual purpose.

Consequently, St. Benedict's double vision attunes him to the rhythm both of creation and of daily life lived in a search for God. Much contemporary spirituality strives for *balance* in life, and the hectic pace of modern life makes it an attractive goal. St. Benedict, however, roots the practices of his *Rule* in a *rhythm* that ebbs and flows according to the demands of the time.

He does this in two basic ways. He establishes a regular rhythm to each day through his careful arrangement of the times for prayer, work, eating, and sleeping. But he also recognizes the rhythms coming from outside his ability to arrange things. So, for example, he says that when the crops are ripe, the monks should occupy themselves with the harvest and know that "when they live by the labor of their hands … then they are really monks" (Chapter 48:8). He recognizes that the daily schedule of the monastery has to change with the seasons, since the monks of his day depended on sunlight and not the local power company!

St. Benedict's openness to the different rhythms of life reveals his mind and how it understood that God makes himself known to us in these rhythms. The emphasis on rhythm offers lessons of patience, of trust, of courage, and of discernment, all of which affect the quality of one's life.

The attention to rhythms of life has struck a chord in many people who, while not professing vows in a monastery, nevertheless find in the *Rule* a voice that speaks to their hearts and a set of practices that pave the avenue for their return to God. St. Benedict recognized the need for a way of life that responded to the deeper desires of the human heart. He says in his *Rule*, "Seeking his workman in a multitude of people, the Lord calls out to him and lifts his voice again, 'Is there anyone here who yearns for life and desires to see good days?'… What, dear brothers, is more delightful than this voice of the Lord calling to us? See how the Lord in His love shows us the way of life" (Prologue 14-15, 19-20).

St. Benedict could not have foreseen just how widely this multitude of people would reach. Although his *Rule* was written for monks living together in a monastery, Christian men and women from many walks in life have come to find in his "little Rule for beginners" a way of wisdom and peace to guide their own search. These everyday people have discovered a treasure of spirituality in monastic practices that they have adapted to their own lives.

## Outer and Inner Rhythms

The present volume takes monastic rhythms as its guiding directive. When Dr. Rowan Williams, the Anglican archbishop of Canterbury, visited Rome in November 2006, his first stop was the Benedictine community at Sant' Anselmo, where he gave a lecture titled "Benedict and the Future of Europe." Dr. Williams noted that one of the things that the *Rule* of Benedict asks is: what is the rhythm of life that best sets a person free to advance to the joy for which we are made?

The authors here offer insights on that important question from several different perspectives. Not all of them are professed monks or nuns, but all of them do share the mind of St. Benedict and seek to make his way their way in accord with their particular state in life. The book is organized according to those "outer rhythms" of *Ora* and *Labora* (Prayer and Work), which govern the rhythm of the day for the life of any Benedictine house; and the "inner rhythms" of the spirit, *Fidelitas* and *Conversatio* (Faithfulness and Conversion).

Fr. Michael Casey, O.C.S.O., begins the *Prayer* section with his reflections on silence as the atmosphere within which the spiritual life can flourish, and Br. Matthew Mattingly, O.S.B., shows how the cherished words of the Psalms have given an audible rhythm to monastic prayer. *Lectio Divina*, the meditative reading of God's Word, is the subject for Fr. Christian Raab, O.S.B., and he shows how this traditional monastic practice opens us to conversation with God. Br. Francis Wagner, O.S.B., rounds out the section on *Prayer* with his reflections on how prayer goes beyond prayers we say and becomes our consciousness of God's presence throughout all our day's activities.

*Work* was important for St. Benedict. Kathleen Norris' contribution points out how our work can become a connection to God's work of creation and thereby our own link to God as creator. Simplicity of life takes a lot of work, and Rev. Dr. Jane Tomaine shows how St. Benedict's way of simplicity puts into practice his admonition to "prefer nothing whatever to Christ." Sr. Joan Chittister, O.S.B., gives the quest for balance a particularly Benedictine focus, seeing it as best achieved in responding to the rhythms of life through trust in God's providence. *Labora* for the disciples of St. Benedict includes the practice of hospitality, and Fr. Meinrad Brune, O.S.B., demonstrates how offering hospitality often breaks our regular rhythms, but in doing so discloses to us the presence of Christ.

For Benedictines, stability is a unique vow. Fr. Joel Rippinger, O.S.B., reflects on how the practices that root us in a given community give expression to the inner rhythm of *Faithfulness*—the theme of the third section of this volume. The *Rule* opens with the word *Listen*, and as Br. Francis shows, listening is a way to grow obedient to the rhythms of life as we discover them in ourselves, in our surroundings, and in others with whom we live. The final two contributions to this section, by Fr. Dwight Longenecker and Sr. Macrina Wiederkehr, O.S.B., give insights on how *Faithfulness* can be lived out in other circles, such as the family and the wide circle of the whole earth.

The last section of the book deals with *Conversion*, not only an inner rhythm, but the means for advancing to that joy for which we are made. Sr. Laura Swan, O.S.B., begins with establishing our relationship with God as the steadying factor among all the changes through which we pass as we go to God. Discretion is indispensible for negotiating the turns on the way to God, and Fr. Harry Hagan, O.S.B., writes about how this virtue pervades the *Rule* and guides one in learning to prefer nothing whatever to Christ. Shedding the weight of self-will frees us for choosing God, and Janis Dopp reflects on how setting aside our own will can open us to a wider range of possibilities in any situation. Finally, Abbot Gregory Polan, O.S.B., explores the supreme paradox of Christianity (and of monastic life): death as the key to unending life. It is the calming of all chaos, the resolution for every rhythm, the gateway to the unending joy for which we are made.

## Where It All Leads

It's not uncommon for us to have a sense of something missing in our lives, a blank spot for something more, despite the many blessings that we do enjoy. There is a deeper desire for something to come along and transform us beyond our present problems and struggles. But we so often settle for far less than what God wants to give us.

The search for God does not necessarily mean living an extraordinary life; it does mean living an ordinary life in an extraordinary way. The practices of monastic life are not so different from the everyday tasks of ordinary people. Those who find a kindred spirit in St. Benedict through his *Rule* strive to share his mind on God, the world, and themselves. And they find in the practices he gave to his monks a way of living their lives in accordance with the spirit of his *Rule*. Those practices put into action the way we understand God, the world, and ourselves.

We do not have to choose between being *spiritual* and being *religious*. A life where desire and practice are inseparably linked in faith is a mindful living in God's presence, embodied in practices. Anyone in any walk of life can step into the rhythms of God and walk toward that joy for which we have all been made—here and now, yes, but also for the life to come.

**Archabbot Justin DuVall, O.S.B.**
*Saint Meinrad Archabbey, July 11, 2011*
*Feast of St. Benedict*

ORA
(PRAY)

"THE ELEVENTH STEP OF HUMILITY
IS THAT WHEN A MONK SPEAKS
HE DOES SO GENTLY AND WITHOUT LAUGHTER,
HUMBLY AND SERIOUSLY, AND THAT HE SAYS
WHAT HE HAS TO IN A FEW REASONABLE WORDS AND
HE DOES NOT SPEAK LOUDLY.
AS IT IS WRITTEN, 'WISE PERSONS ARE KNOWN
FOR THE FEWNESS OF THEIR WORDS.' "

— *Rule of St. Benedict, Ch. 7:60-61*

# Listening To God

## The Value Of Silence In The Spiritual Life

***by Fr. Michael Casey, O.C.S.O.***

Have you ever looked around at your fellow passengers as a newly landed plane begins to taxi toward the terminal? Many of them are reaching for their cell phones. When the screen lights up, so do their faces in anticipation. If there are messages for them, all is well; if not, they snap the phone shut and dolefully return it to its place.

We live in a world in which communication is highly valued, and its absence seems like an indicator of our little worth. It is as though the various means of communication are elements in our life-support system. Unless we remain connected to them we cease to exist. The content of the communication seems to matter less than the fact that somebody out there acknowledges our existence and wishes to make contact with us.

Granted the importance of communication and the anxiety we experience in its absence, why does St. Benedict regard silence as such an important element in leading a serious spiritual life?

## Sins of the Tongue

In his usual blunt way Benedict reminds us, first of all, that "in much speaking you will not avoid sinning" (Proverbs 10:19). It is a common observation that religious people express their resistance to God and their detachment from their neighbor less by overt actions than by thoughts and in their conversation. It is almost as though the evil within them, that they are trying to suppress by being good, somehow escapes despite their best efforts. Saint James devotes the third chapter of his Epistle to this theme and concludes that those who have reached the point of being able to control their tongues are already perfect (James 3:2).

The effort to monitor our speech is a good indication that we are serious about the spiritual life and that we have begun to live by some form of personal discipline. A refusal to be complicit in gossip, detraction, and slander is likely to change for the better the quality of our interaction with others and improve our peace of heart.

"HUMAN MISFORTUNE COMES ENTIRELY FROM A SINGLE CAUSE: NOT KNOWING HOW TO SIT QUIETLY IN A ROOM."

— *Blaise Pascal*

The laborious struggle to hold our tongue may also lead us in the direction of useful self-scrutiny. Why do we feel the need to talk so much? Why is it so hard to stop bad-mouthing others? Why are we so lacking in empathy that we are constantly harping on deficiencies?

If we sin often by speaking, then we will sin less often by speaking less.

# Absence of Noise

Monasteries are typically built in areas that are somewhat remote from the bustle of city life. Within the monastic environment, there is a conscious effort to do things with a minimum of noise. People visiting a monastery are often surprised by the quiet: they can hear the birds singing or the rustle of the trees in the wind.

Some are delighted, but others are disoriented, so accustomed are they to a constant background of noise: traffic, machinery, television, conversation.

Silence invites us to give less attention to the external world and to become more aware of the inner world, the world of spirit. We are able to hear the voice of conscience, and we become more aware of the Holy Spirit's interior guidance. Prayer comes more easily because we are less distracted by extraneous sounds. This is why silence is a favored element of a prayerful retreat.

Silence can also be uncomfortable and even frightening. Because of this, we like to surround ourselves with familiar sounds. When we are quiet and still, the inner voices that are kept at bay by noise and activity begin to speak, and what they have to say to us is not always welcome.

Sometimes we discover within ourselves tendencies and desires that run contrary to the chosen direction of our life. In the same way, silence reveals to us what has yet to be done if our spiritual life is to be real. A recent reality TV program exploring this dimension provided this observation: "What's happening in the silence is that stuff is coming up that I normally don't give attention to, and I can get ambushed."

The ancient monks went out into the desert to engage in spiritual warfare. Their experience was that where there is no distraction, it is impossible to avoid or postpone the inevitable clash with the negative elements in our own nature and history. Without a good measure of silence we will be merely skimming the surface of the spiritual life—doing good deeds and practicing the virtues—without ever scrutinizing the motives and intentions that inspire them. And, from time to time, we will be shocked when we behave in a way that is inconsistent with our ideals. We will be puzzled why this should be so.

A quiet and unexciting ambience is a valuable adjunct to our efforts to live spiritually. And if we cannot live thus always, there is an advantage in regularly seeking to withdraw from the noise and bustle of ordinary life into a zone of silence in which we can add depth to the spiritual pursuit.

To live sociably among others, it is necessary sometimes to be solitary. To engage fruitfully in conversation, it is necessary to develop the art of sometimes remaining silent.

## Restraint of Speech

Saint Benedict uses two different Latin words which are both often translated as "silence." One is *silentium,* in which the emphasis is on an absence of noise. The other is *taciturnitas,* which properly means restraint of speech or taciturnity.

In his *Rule,* Benedict is quite severe in asking his disciples to curb their speech: "Because of the seriousness of silence, permission to speak should be given rarely to advanced disciples even for good and holy words of edification." Benedict wants his monks to speak sparingly and to listen willingly, to fill their waking hours with the praise of God, purposeful work, assiduous reading and prayerful rumination. He puts in place rules of silence to restrict speech to specific times and places, so as to make possible the enjoyment of solitude even in a large and industrious community.

Small talk, idle chatter, and jokes he bans completely—though we may be allowed to wonder how successful this prohibition actually was!

It has to be remembered that St. Benedict lived in an oral/aural culture in which most of his monks would have had an instinctive preference for verbal communication over reading from books. To make provision for substantial and ongoing contact with the beliefs and values of monastic tradition, times for reading and reflection had to be protected. He even designated a couple of senior monks to patrol the monastery during periods of reading to make sure that slackers would not waste their time in meaningless conversation.

Silence is at the service of *lectio divina* (sacred, prayerful reading) and its kindred activities. Keeping silence for the sake of silence is meaningless. We restrain ourselves from speaking in order to listen. Only when we stop talking can we hear what others are saying.

To devote ourselves assiduously to sacred reading we need a time and space that is conducive to paying attention. Only when we are silent can we pass into deeper reflection: we cannot ponder and talk at the same time. Silence is necessary if we are to be aware of our conscience, of the interior promptings of the Holy Spirit, of the profound stirrings of our own spirits as they are drawn into prayer.

Without some measure of silence nothing much happens in our spiritual lives; we may do good deeds and practice virtue but our contact with the spiritual world will be slight, and our sense of intimacy with God undernourished.

Restraint of speech is an element in personal discipline which enables us to use our time wisely, but it is more than that. It is the means by which we are more receptive to other persons and to God. It is the necessary condition by which the Word of God implants itself in our heart, matures, and bears fruit. Without silence there is no growth in wisdom since, as St. Benedict reminds us, "Wise persons are known for the fewness of their words."

# Quality Conversation

When our speech is under discipline it is far more likely to be encouraging and instructive to others, less prone to sowing the seeds of dissension, and more effective as a vehicle for transmitting the wisdom slowly acquired through long experience. Above all, such interior silence that expresses itself through outward attentiveness makes a person a ready listener, able not only to hear what is said but to perceive what is meant and to have some appreciation of the inner state of the one who speaks.

To arrive at such a state requires much self-restraint animated by a sincere concern to listen to others sympathetically. To welcome what others have to say is to offer a rare form of hospitality. Good listening is the most sincere form of kindness and the supreme mark of honor that we can give another.

The other person is not the only beneficiary, as we know from our own experience. If we set ourselves the task of really listening, we will often hear a word that touches us powerfully, whether as a comfort or a challenge. Nothing is more certain than the fact that God speaks to us through human agencies, but in a very subtle way. Unless we listen carefully we may miss the message. When mature Christians engage in mutual listening Christ is present.

## Mystical Silence

Silence not only provides the environment for prayer, it progressively becomes the *content* of prayer. Monastic prayer is an attentive and respectful stilling of the voice, the imagination, and the mind in anticipation of the Lord's presence, slowly revealed. As prayer develops it tends to become less wordy until, at last, it needs only a few words to frame it. Sometimes "there is silence in heaven for half an hour" (Revelation 8:1).

The monastic tradition insists this is a relatively rare experience, especially in the beginning. More often than not the silence experienced in prayer is the simple act of waiting for the body and mind to become still so that God's voice may be more clearly heard. Then we keep watch for the Lord's coming. We pray not with many words, as St. Benedict says, but with tears of compunction and heartfelt desire.

## Listening with the Ear of the Heart

1. *The gift of a highly developed language sets human beings apart from the animal world. Why restrict it?*

2. *How is it possible to incorporate the value of silence into our lives when we live in a world of which constant communication is an essential part?*

3. *Examine your experience when you have made a conscious choice to refrain from uncharitable words or mindless banter. What fruit followed such a choice?*

"[DURING LENT] LET THE EAR FAST
FROM ITS EVIL ITCH TO LISTEN TO STORIES
AND RUMORS AND WHATEVER IS UNPROFITABLE
OR HAS LITTLE BEARING ON SALVATION.
LET THE TONGUE FAST FROM DETRACTION
AND GRUMBLING, FROM USELESS, VAIN, AND
SCURRILOUS WORDS, AND—BECAUSE OF THE
SERIOUSNESS OF SILENCE—SOMETIMES EVEN
WORDS THAT COULD BE NECESSARY."

*— St. Bernard of Clairvaux*

"MONKS WHO IN A WEEK'S TIME
RECITE LESS THAN THE ENTIRE PSALTER
AND THE ESTABLISHED RESPONSES,
BETRAY THEMSELVES AS LACKING
IN THEIR DEVOTION, FOR WE READ,
AFTER ALL, THAT OUR HOLY FATHERS
IN THEIR ZEAL ACCOMPLISHED
THIS IN A SINGLE DAY."

— *Rule of St. Benedict, Ch. 18:24-25*

# The Psalms as Soul Food

## A Pattern of Prayer for Life

***By Br. Matthew Mattingly, O.S.B.***

In 2009, my monastery witnessed the passing of Fr. Theodore Heck, O.S.B., a faithful monk who lived to be 108 years old—85 of those as a member of our community. At his wake, as we were chanting the Psalms during the Divine Office for the Dead, I wondered how many times he had prayed those same psalms during the course of his life, as the *Rule* of St. Benedict recommends praying the Psalter on a weekly cycle.

Later, out of curiosity, I did the math and estimated that he would have gone through the entire Psalter—all 150 psalms—well over 2,000 times! This number does not include individual psalms he would have said at Mass or during private devotion. Whatever the actual figure, this is a tremendous number of times to have recited or sung one body of literature over a lifetime.

It is impossible to estimate the effects that such devotion to a single text has on the makeup of a person, and how much it contributes to forming and shaping his or her character. This is especially so when we consider that the Book of Psalms is not just any text, but the very words of God himself.

## Food for the Journey

In his book *Bread in the Wilderness,* Trappist monk and author Thomas Merton compares the Psalms to the manna with which God provided the Israelites as they made their 40-year journey through the desert to the Promised Land. In making this connection, Merton stands within a long tradition that reaches back to the Fathers of the Church, and is rooted in Jesus' own teaching.

If materially our physical bodies are a reflection of what we put into them—of the food that we eat—so, too, are our souls ultimately a reflection of what we feed them in the more figurative sense. Surely it is no accident that the common thread tying together that diverse and varied group known as the communion of saints is a lifetime of praying and being formed by the Book of Psalms.

Fr. Theodore is unique only in his longevity and the duration of his devotion to the Psalms. The pattern of prayer that shaped his life is no different than that which has shaped the lives of countless monks and nuns for more than 1,500 years. It is impossible to over-exaggerate the power and influence this collection of ancient prayers has had—and continues to have—on the life of individuals, the universal Church, and the world at large.

"FOR THE MONK WHO REALLY ENTERS INTO THE FULL MEANING OF HIS VOCATION, THE PSALMS ARE THE NOURISHMENT OF HIS INTERIOR LIFE … SO THAT AT LAST HE COMES TO LIVE THEM AND EXPERIENCE THEM AS IF THEY WERE HIS OWN SONGS, HIS OWN PRAYERS."

— *Thomas Merton*

# Human Hunger For God

What exactly is a psalm? It is not a word we hear much, if at all, apart from the context of the Bible or the liturgy. This seems fitting, for there is nothing quite like the Psalms. At one and the same time they are poems, hymns, prayers, and prophecies. They seem to have a unique sound, a rhythm, and language all their own.

When we hear the word "psalm" we immediately think of the Book of Psalms of the Old Testament, but in the Bible the word is not limited to this collection. There are numerous examples of psalms scattered throughout the pages of Sacred Scripture. They seem to appear at all the great moments of salvation history. Moses and the Israelites spontaneously sing a great psalm of praise after being delivered from slavery in Egypt, as does King David when the Ark of the Covenant enters Jerusalem; barren Hannah, mother of the prophet Samuel, offers a psalm of thanksgiving after learning of her long-awaited pregnancy; we find the Virgin Mary doing the same following the Annunciation. There are many more such examples.

Essentially, the Psalms and their poetic structure are intended to convey what no other form of human language is capable of fully expressing: the profound experience of God's mercy, justice, and salvation at the deepest and most personal level.

Not all the Psalms, however, are songs of praise or thanksgiving. In fact, the majority in the Book of Psalms are classified as laments—songs of anguish and despair. Just as poetic language best captures the experience of the divine presence, so, too, that of God's perceived absence.

Many who approach the Book of Psalms for the first time are often shocked, even offended, by the raw language used in many of the laments. We are not comfortable with such language; we typically judge it unworthy of prayer addressed to God. Yet, there it is, right in the heart of Scripture. How are we to make sense of this?

We must always keep in mind the tragic history of ancient Israel which forms the context out of which the Psalms arose. These are the prayers of King David as he finds himself pursued by bloodthirsty enemies, including his own son; they are those of a people who witnessed their beloved Jerusalem burned to the ground, their homes destroyed, the sources of their livelihood laid waste; they are the laments of those who had to endure a generation of bitter exile in Babylon.

The Psalms are the prayers of people who have had to suffer much. From this standpoint their vengeful tone, if not wholly acceptable, is at least understandable. It may be edifying to note, however, that the psalmists do not take it upon themselves to carry out the violence their prayers often call for; rather it is from God that they seek their justice. We find Israel waiting, albeit at times impatiently, for God to hear their prayers, to remain true to the promise made to God's chosen people. Ultimately, such lamenting is a sign of hope, for one who does not expect to be heard (and therefore lacks hope) does not cry out at all.

## Christ, the Bread of Life

It is against this backdrop that we understand Christ to be God's answer to the Old Testament prayers articulated in the Psalms. The New Testament is full of references to them; in the gospels Jesus cites them frequently; the account of his Passion is by and large framed in their language. When Jesus cries out from the cross, "My God, my God, why have you forsaken me?" quoting the opening line of Psalm 22, it is as if at that moment he is taking upon himself the whole history of Israel's suffering and sense of abandonment as expressed in the lamentations of the Psalms, and with his final breath offering them up collectively to God the Father.

It is in Christ that we see the fulfillment of the Psalms. They refer to him, they look forward to him, and they take their meaning from him. The Church Fathers were insistent on this point. In assuming these prayers, Jesus also transforms them; he fulfills them in a way that is unexpected.

The original psalmists, in their cries for justice, had prayed for their enemies to be destroyed. Christ, however, reveals that God's idea of justice is not the same as ours. "Forgive them, Father," he prays from the cross, "for they know not what they do."

Because Christ made these psalms his own prayer while at the same time fulfilling them, they are not merely the prayers of an ancient people, but belong to each and every one of us as the Body of Christ. They have become the most fitting form of prayer for all Christians crying out from the cross.

# Praying with Christ

In the Catholic tradition, many associate the liturgy with the Mass, the celebration of the Eucharist, and this is indeed its "source and summit." However, the liturgy extends further than this, and it is rooted in the Psalms. Each day monks, nuns, priests, and other religious, as well as many lay people and Christians from other traditions, join their voices in praying the Liturgy of the Hours (also known as the Divine Office). This is the great common prayer of the universal Church.

It is called the Liturgy of the Hours because it is prayed at certain times throughout the day—the morning prayer of Lauds and the evening prayer of Vespers being the most prominent. It is composed of hymns, antiphons, responsories, and readings which mark the days of the liturgical year, but it is the Psalms that serve as its foundation. The entire Psalter is either recited or chanted over the course of a four-week cycle.

To pray the Psalter is to pray in Christ's own words. It is to join ourselves to his sufferings just as he joined himself to the sufferings of Israel. It is to join ourselves in Christ to the prayers of all those who suffer in the world today; it is to make their suffering our suffering. It is to pray for the full realization of Christ's triumph in all souls and throughout the world.

To do so is to share in Christ's priesthood. Ultimately, this is what forms the Church; this is what makes communion possible; this is what prepares us to share in the joy of his Resurrection.

# Shaped by God's Word

In his *Rule,* St. Benedict calls the act of praying the Liturgy of the Hours the "Work of God." This is true in the sense that it fulfills our obligation to God to render praise and worship. Perhaps most fittingly, however, it is understood to be the work that God performs on us. It is through the daily commitment of praying the Psalms that we allow God to finish the work of creation in us.

When one prays the Psalms for a long period of time, day after day, week after week, year after year, they slowly start to become part of you. You begin to memorize them; you find the words and phrases of these ancient prayers becoming a part of your own private prayer, until one day you reach the point where the Psalms simply are your prayer—you no longer have to make anything up. The words you need are just there, and it is God who has supplied them.

In praying the Psalms we come to share in the mind of Christ. Already made in his image, we come more perfectly to realize his likeness.

It is unlikely that Fr. Theodore will ever officially be declared a saint. Still, all of us who lived with him or knew him found inspiration and edification in his humble dignity, kind words, and faithful perseverance. His life, indeed, shaped as it was by the Psalms, bears witness to the power of prayer to change lives and its vital necessity for building up the Church on earth.

## Listening with the Ear of the Heart

*Almighty and merciful God,*
*in giving us the Book of Psalms you revealed to your Church*
*a window into the mind of your Son, Jesus Christ.*
*May our devotion to their recital and prayer*
*make our hearts and minds one with his,*
*so that we and your Church might experience in time*
*the fullness of his Incarnation.*

"WHEN WE COME TO HAVE
THE SAME DISPOSITION IN OUR HEART
WITH WHICH EACH PSALM WAS SUNG
OR WRITTEN DOWN, THEN WE SHALL
HAVE BECOME LIKE ITS AUTHOR,
GRASPING ITS MEANING BEFOREHAND."

— *John Cassian*

"WHAT PAGE, WHAT PASSAGE
OF THE INSPIRED BOOKS
OF THE OLD AND NEW TESTAMENTS
IS NOT THE TRUEST OF GUIDES
FOR HUMAN LIFE?"

— *Rule of St. Benedict, Ch. 73:3*

# A Guide to Lectio Divina
## God's Word Made Alive

***by Fr. Christian Raab, O.S.B.***

My brother had a funny way of watching television when we were kids. During the show "Kung Fu," he would run to his bedroom, put on a bathrobe—tied tight around the waist to look like a kimono—and return. Then he would begin punching and kicking in imitation of the images he saw on the screen.

When a football game was on, he would don a football uniform—complete with shoulder pads—and tackle pillows. He was so excited about what he saw on TV that he had to make it real, bring it to life.

This is very similar to the way early monks read Scripture (without the punching, kicking, or tackling). They encountered an image on the page or heard a word proclaimed to them, and felt inspired—almost compelled—to make it real. They wanted to have the Word become flesh in them.

A famous example is that of St. Anthony of the Desert, considered the founder of monasticism. A young Anthony heard the story of the rich young man proclaimed in church. A phrase stuck out to him: "If you wish to be perfect, go, sell what you have and give it to the poor, and you will have treasure in heaven. Then come, follow me" (Matthew 19:21). Inspired by the Holy Spirit, St. Anthony responded by selling his possessions, giving the proceeds to the poor, and venturing into the desert to live a life of prayer. He received the Word and brought it to life.

When St. Benedict wrote his *Rule* for monks, he built into the day periods for *lectio divina,* or sacred reading. Through a daily routine of communal liturgy and personal *lectio,* the monks continuously embraced the Word of God—which would sometimes console, sometimes challenge, and hopefully always inspire them toward holiness.

However, monks are not the only ones who practice *lectio divina.* For Christians anywhere, it is a tried and true guide for life and a privileged place to encounter God in prayer.

"THE FRUIT OF LECTIO DIVINA IS A CONSCIOUS, LIVING, AND ACTIVE RELATIONSHIP WITH GOD."

— *Mary Margaret Funk, O.S.B.*

# The Practice of Lectio Divina

In practicing *lectio divina,* it is important to keep some things in mind and some things at heart.

### *Things to keep in mind*

The Scriptures were written long ago, and contain much that is confusing—even frustrating—to our modern eyes and ears. Contemporary scholars emphasize that we view the Scriptures through the lens of our own particular history, culture, and context. As such, it is necessary to consider what the Scriptures may have meant to their original human authors. We can ask whether a particular text was originally intended as a history (like a news report), or whether it was written in the language of prayer or poetry. Since the Bible is full of many different types of literature, it is important to keep that question front and center.

Likewise, to grasp the meaning of Scripture passages more fully, it is helpful to discuss them with others who may have a different point of view, consult commentaries, or see how the saints or other figures from the Christian tradition viewed a particular passage.

**Four Senses of Scripture:** The Church Fathers maintained that any piece of Scripture can say many things at once. They believed one should consider it from different vantage points. One good illustration of this concept is the ancient story from India about a group of blind men examining an elephant. One blind man holding the elephant's tail thought it was like a rope. The one touching the leg thought it was like a tree. The one holding the ear thought it was like a sail. The one stroking the tusk imagined that it was like a spear. They were all right—and they were all wrong because each had only one point of view.

The early monastics knew that there is more than one meaning to a story, and that to get the full meaning, one needs to view it from many directions. So, they identified four layers of meaning in Scripture: **literal, allegorical, moral, and mystical**.

The **literal** meaning of a Scripture is its most evident meaning. On its surface, the story of Moses leading the Hebrews across the Red Sea into the Promised Land is an epic tale of an ancient prophet leading an enslaved people out of bondage.

The **allegorical** meaning refers to the way in which the text points to the life of Christ or the life of the Church. The Exodus story can be read as a symbolic narrative pointing to the way God's people would be brought through the waters of baptism into salvation.

The **moral** meaning refers to the way the listener should personally respond to the story. In its moral meaning, the Exodus story instructs the reader to flee the slavery of sin (represented by Egypt) and follow Christ (symbolized by Moses).

The **mystical** meaning of a text refers to eternal life. In this sense, the waters of the Red Sea are the waters of judgment that sweep away the old world. The land of Canaan toward which the Israelites are headed is heaven, or life in God.

### *Things to keep at heart*

The monastic tradition suggests three things to keep at heart while reading Scripture: **faith, silence,** and **openness**.

Perhaps the greatest difference between reading the Bible and reading a story in a newspaper is that, as people of **faith**, we believe that God—the Divine author—is really with us when we read Scripture in a way that the human author of a newspaper story is not. The first thing to keep at heart when we read the Bible is the faith that God is really there with us, that God knows we are reading, and that God speaks to us through the Word.

The second thing to keep at heart is **silence**. The famous story of Elijah the prophet tells us that God speaks to us in a silent whisper (1 Kings 19:12). We need to clear away some of the clutter and busyness in our lives so that we can hear God speak in the Scriptures.

The third thing to keep at heart is **openness**. God intends our encounter with the Word to change us. Mary has long been the symbol of openness to God. Medieval paintings depict her with Scripture in hand at the time of the Annunciation. The idea behind these images is that Mary was so open to God's Word that the Word was able to become flesh in her. Likewise, God desires to become flesh in us.

So, like my brother watching television, we must be open and willing to let the image of God come to life in us.

## Practical Matters

With all these things in mind and at heart, how do we begin *lectio divina,* and what do we do? Here are a few short answers.

### *Who?*

*Lectio divina* is about a relationship between God and us. When we sit down to *lectio*, we recall that we are in the presence of the One who loves us and who knows us better than we even know ourselves. Through the Word, God is revealed to us. Furthermore, God reveals us to ourselves, since the seed of the Word is already in our hearts. God wakes up our potential and comes to life in our humanity.

## *What?*

Scripture should be the beginning point for *lectio divina*. It is possible to practice *lectio* with other material—such as devotional books or the lives of the saints—since God is revealed in many ways. However, a regular diet of Scripture should be maintained. It can be added to, but not abandoned.

The monastic tradition recommends picking a book of the Bible and slowly working through it from beginning to end. Another possibility is to use daily liturgical readings. In any case, it is not typically helpful to choose passages at random. In doing that, one usually gravitates toward favorite passages. Then, is God speaking—or am I making God say what I want to hear?

## *Where?*

Because of the importance of silence, it is often helpful to find a quiet place to read. Churches are perfect, but one can also read on a park bench, or in one's bedroom.

## *When?*

Establish a routine period. Make it the same time every day, and remain committed to it. Like a physical fitness program, *lectio* will only be fruitful if we stick with it—not just when we feel like it. St. Benedict reserved the earliest part of the day for this practice, when the mind is most alert.

## *How?*

In the Middle Ages, a four-step method was developed for *lectio divina*. The stages are: ***lectio*** (reading), ***meditatio*** (meditation), ***oratio*** (prayer), and ***contemplatio*** (contemplation).

*Begin with a prayer to the Holy Spirit to aid your reading. Then:*

***Lectio:*** Read the passage twice through. This encounter is like meeting someone for the first time. Initially, you only notice superficial things like glasses or the color of clothing. As you read through a second time remember any word or phrase or image that sticks out to you. Pause at the end of your reading for a few minutes and repeat the word or phrase in your mind.

***Meditatio:*** Read through the passage again. At the end of your reading pause for several minutes and reflect upon what God seems to be saying to you through the text. Is the Word speaking to you about your relationship with God, or with others, or with yourself? Is God consoling you? Challenging you? Inspiring you?

***Oratio:*** Read through the passage again. At the end of your reading stop for several minutes and collect a prayer to return to God. What do you need to say to God in response to the Word? Each time will be different. You may feel prompted to ask for help (for yourself or for someone else), to give God thanks, to seek forgiveness, to do something, or simply to give praise to Our Lord.

***Contemplatio:*** Read through the passage one final time. Then, simply sit quietly in the presence of God. Imagine an old married couple (*happily* married!) who can simply enjoy being in the presence of one another without speaking. That is contemplation!

*Finish with an Our Father or some other prayer.*

# Conversation with God

Does the prayer of *lectio divina* seem like a conversation? *That's what it is!* In this conversation, God speaks, we listen, and then we respond.

Our relationship with the Lord deepens through *lectio divina*. It engages the mind and heart in a relationship with the living God who speaks to us. It is a great way to grow closer to God and to bring the Word to life—to make it real, to allow God to become flesh in our daily lives.

Bathrobes or shoulder pads are optional!

# Listening with the Ear of the Heart

1. *Is there a Scripture story that you find particularly appealing? Why do you think that is? How does it come alive in your life?*

2. *What would be the best time of your day to set aside for lectio divina? Where would you do it?*

“HOLY WRIT IS SET BEFORE THE EYES
OF THE MIND LIKE A KIND OF MIRROR,
THAT WE MAY SEE OUR INWARD FACE IN IT;
FOR THEREIN WE LEARN THE DEFORMITIES,
THEREIN WE LEARN THE BEAUTIES
THAT WE POSSESS;
THERE WE ARE MADE SENSIBLE
TO WHAT PROGRESS WE ARE MAKING,
THERE TOO HOW FAR WE ARE
FROM PROFICIENCY.”

*— Gregory the Great*

"PRAYER SHOULD BE SHORT AND PURE, UNLESS PERHAPS IT IS PROLONGED UNDER THE INSPIRATION OF DIVINE GRACE."

— *Rule of St. Benedict, Ch. 20:4*

# Invitation to Prayer:
## Time and Being with God

***By Br. Francis de Sales Wagner, O.S.B.***

Sitting behind me in the chapel were a young woman and her 4-year-old daughter. I met them on the way in, wondering (selfishly) how I was going to pray with a restless child in our midst.

The girl was trying her best to remain still, leafing through a prayer book. As the minutes stretched the youngster's attention span to its limits, she began turning the pages more briskly, drawing gentle reminders from her mother of the need for quiet. The child was eager to obey, but simply unable to help herself.

As the two prepared to leave, the woman asked her daughter if she had anything to say to God.

Suddenly, this child's profound simplicity and confidence in God filled the entire chapel. Kneeling, she began praising God with a love and devotion beyond description, lifting her voice to heaven for 20 seconds of eternity. I began to smile. The child's mother was sobbing with joy.

For close to an hour, two adults attempted to teach this child how to pray. Instead, in 20 seconds, she taught us what it means to be truly immersed in God's presence—not with lofty words, but with her entire being. She approached God simply as she was.

God's presence in our lives must be acknowledged with the heart of a child. That doesn't mean we must pray like a 4-year-old does. However, what the girl in the chapel offered to God is what we are *all* called to offer. God wants our *time* and our *being* in it.

# What Is Prayer?

Prayer is God's **invitation** to **dedicate** our time and being to a fuller **appreciation** of the divine so that our vision broadens and our hearts **expand** through Love. It is a life-long rhythm of listening and responding to God's call for conversion of heart — personally and communally.

St. Benedict offers us a time-honored approach to an integrated life of prayer. In his Rule for monks, he does not present a complex theory on contemplation. Rather, he sketches a practical and adaptable framework for those living in the monastery (or outside it) to center time and being in God's presence — in prayer, work, and community living.

"GOD PROVIDES FOR US IN SURPRISING WAYS EACH DAY, WHICH GIVES US HOPE. OUR LIFE OF PRAYER IS WHAT SHINES THE LIGHT ON THIS HOPE EACH DAY. IT IS HOW GOD TALKS TO US."

*— Fr. Theodore Heck, O.S.B., Saint Meinrad Archabbey 1901–2009*

On one point he is very clear: We *respond*, but first we *listen*. "Listen carefully, my child, to the teacher's instructions, and attend to them with the ear of your heart," St. Benedict says in the Prologue of the Rule. "First of all, you must pray to God most earnestly to bring every good work to perfection."

We are to listen like children within our hearts to what the Gospel has to teach us. We pray, and then we work, and we pray again — all for the love of Christ.

"Prayer lies at the very heart of the Benedictine life," says Esther de Waal in *Seeking God: The Way of St. Benedict*. "It holds everything together, it sustains every other activity. It is at the same time root and fruit, foundation and fulfillment. Praying can never be set apart from the rest of life; it is life itself."

So, prayer is at the heart of life, and life is at the heart of prayer. It is an intentional offering of time and being for no other purpose than praise of God. The key word is intentional. For those living out a monastic vocation, this *intentional* offering is anchored by three traditions: liturgical prayer (the Eucharist and Divine Office, or Work of God), *lectio divina* (prayerful reading of Scripture and other spiritual texts), and work. All other aspects of monastic life course through and from this triple foundation.

While the monastic life is a specific call to intentionally seek God, St. Benedict offers a framework for *anyone* wishing to dedicate time and being to God. You don't have to be a monk to pray, although it may help to know how a monk approaches prayer.

## Invitation

Prayer is a pure gift that cannot be truly appreciated unless it is truly received. Receiving this gift doesn't require anything more than a heart receptive to the Word of God. We are called to open the door and invite the gift that invites us to deeper union with God.

"Come away to a deserted place all by yourselves and rest a while," Jesus tells us (Mark 6:31). "The Lord your God is with you … He will quiet you with his love" (Zephaniah 3:17). "Be still and know that I am God" (Psalm 46:10).

These are but a few examples of God's invitation to pray, to listen. The "deserted place" of which Christ speaks is one's heart. Prayer is a time to rest in God as a child rests in its mother's arms. It is a time apart to settle into hearing God's Word. "Speaking and teaching are the master's task," St. Benedict tells us. "The disciple is to be silent and listen."

In the monastery each day, monks arise before dawn and keep silence until the bells summon everyone into the church to chant the Divine Office for Vigils and Lauds. The first words spoken for the day are in unison and directed toward God: "O Lord, open my lips and my mouth shall proclaim your praise" (Psalm 51:17).

Before any business or conversation for the day is conducted, the monk is immersed in God's Word so that it may shape his prayer, work, and community life. At regular intervals throughout each day, the monk returns to this time of prayer to listen to God — in the spoken Word, and in the depths of his heart.

People in many walks of life and from many faith traditions have prayed this way for thousands of years, centering personal and liturgical worship in the psalms and Scripture. That kind of staying power has a message for us all. Monk or not, all are invited to listen to the Word.

# Dedication

"Nothing is to be preferred to the Work of God," St. Benedict says. Prayer is the first and last work of the day, and what guides, sustains, and completes all other work.

This means consecrating — or setting apart — a specific time and place to pray, as well as offering shorter moments of prayer throughout the day. Just like following through on a fitness program, it means dedicating oneself to a plan of action and carrying it out, day after day. Slowly but surely, it becomes part of us, reshapes who we are, and flows out to encompass all of life.

Approaches can vary. For instance, one might dedicate 30 minutes in the morning to prayerful reading of a psalm or Gospel passage, set aside 10 minutes at lunch to silently thank God, and devote another 20 minutes in the evening to spiritual reading. Many lay people pray the Divine Office daily, and engage God through monastic practices such as *lectio divina*.

This life of prayer must be intentional and consistent, a complete dedication of time and being with God. The key is to establish a pattern and abide by it, resisting (within reason, of course) the urge to make revisions to suit momentary preferences. When the bell rings for prayer, the faithful monk goes, no matter what he is doing, because *nothing* is to be preferred to the Work of God.

When we give God our time and being before all else, we make good use of the gift of prayer, no matter how unappealing, difficult, or pointless it may seem at the moment. As Fr. Hilary Ottensmeyer, a deceased monk of Saint Meinrad Archabbey said, "Until you are convinced that prayer is the best use of your time, you will not find the time for prayer."

## Appreciation and Vision

Here, the real work begins—on us, not by us. As St. Paul says, the Spirit "comes to the aid of our weakness; for we do not know how to pray as we ought ... The one who searches hearts knows what is the intention of the Spirit, because it intercedes for the holy ones according to God's will" (Romans 8:26-27).

Over time, prayer permeates the day. As we digest God's Word in prayer, it begins to nourish and reshape us, drawing connections with the events and relationships in our lives. Then, guided by the Spirit we become the Word in action.

With regular prayer rooted in the psalms and Scripture, we don't get to pick and choose to suit moods, perceived circumstances, and agendas. God's Word is there before us, and in it we are confronted with ourselves and extended beyond ourselves into the life of the wider church and world. "There is no Christianity that consists only of the individual believer and God," says Roberta Bondi, a professor of church history and author on monastic topics.

St. Benedict knew this well. Time and being with God in regular personal and liturgical prayer gradually deepens our appreciation of the divine presence at all times and in everything and everyone. It sharpens our vision in this journey toward our heavenly home, and offers us moments of grace along the way.

"We believe that the divine presence is everywhere. This is especially true when we celebrate the Divine Office," St. Benedict says. This is the fountain from which our conversion of heart drinks. True prayer, after all, is not a relaxation technique, a personal "wish list," or a manufactured experience of bliss. It is being with God who is present to one and all — not so we can get things we want, but so we are conformed to Christ.

## Expansion

What St. Benedict offers is a Gospel-centered life of prayer that is attentive to *all* the ways God is present to us, so that we become more fully present to God in every aspect of our lives. As Benedictine Sister Mary Forman notes, prayer's aim is the "widening of one's vision such that one begins to see as God sees, to love all that God has created as God has, to view life's situations as God does."

The girl in the chapel possessed this vision. She gave God her time and being. Like a songbird announcing the dawn, the words of the spontaneous psalm that poured forth from her lips welled up from an expanded heart bursting with pure love of God the Father.

This child hungered for God. Her prayer was urgent, yet exuberant, caught up in a moment transcending time. This hunger for God is what nourishes all of life. It invites us to pray because life depends on it.

When we respond to this invitation, St. Benedict tells us, and faithfully dedicate our time and being to God, "we shall run on the path of God's commands, our hearts expanded with the inexpressible delight of love."

## Listening with the Ear of the Heart

1. *Is prayer at the heart of my life? If so, how may it be deepened? If not, what stands in the way? How might God be extending an invitation to be silent and listen with the "ear of my heart?"*

2. *What are some practical changes I can make to more fully dedicate my time and being to God in prayer, work, and community life (family, neighborhood, church, etc.)?*

3. *What do I want from God? What does God want from me? How might my personal and liturgical prayer deepen my appreciation of the divine and sharpen my vision of God's presence in my life … in the lives of those around me … in the world?*

4. *What does my life depend on? Where is my heart, and is it expanding?*

"THE HIGHEST GOOD IS PRAYER
AND CONVERSATION WITH GOD,
BECAUSE IT MEANS THAT
WE ARE IN GOD'S COMPANY
AND IN UNION WITH HIM.
WHEN LIGHT ENTERS OUR BODILY EYES,
OUR EYESIGHT IS SHARPENED;
WHEN A SOUL IS INTENT ON GOD,
GOD'S INEXTINGUISHABLE LIGHT
SHINES INTO IT AND MAKES IT BRIGHT
AND CLEAR. I AM TALKING,
OF COURSE, OF PRAYER THAT
COMES FROM THE HEART."

— *St. John Chrysostom*

# LABORA
## (WORK)

"IDLENESS IS THE ENEMY OF THE SOUL.
THEREFORE, THE BROTHERS
SHOULD HAVE SPECIFIED PERIODS
FOR MANUAL LABOR
AS WELL AS PRAYERFUL READING."

— *Rule of St. Benedict, Ch. 48:1*

# Making Our Work Holy

## Reconnecting with God the Creator

***by Kathleen Norris***

How would Adam approach the idea of making work holy, upon hearing, "Cursed is the ground because of you; in toil you shall eat of it all the days of your life. … By the sweat of your face you shall eat bread until you return to the ground, for out of it you were taken, you are dust" (Genesis 3:17b-19)? Could Adam envision the alarm buzzing at 6 a.m., the daily commute fueled by caffeine and road rage? Or did he foresee something even worse: sweating in the fields as an exploited migrant laborer or breathing toxic fumes in a factory? Work as dead-end stuff: dirty, dusty days leading inexorably back to dust.

Eve is another matter, and irony is at the heart of it: "I will greatly increase your pangs in childbearing; in pain you shall bring forth children, yet your desire shall be for your husband, and he shall rule over you" (Genesis 3:16). Her "work" is to be a child-bearer, wife, and helpmate. But just ask a new mother if all the pain of pregnancy and labor was worth it. Chances are she is still rapt in wonder over this creature she has brought into the world. As for having Adam "rule" over her, well, in her dialogue with the serpent, Eve has proved herself a good theologian, and a master of irony. She'll figure it out, and with Adam, build a home and family. Work as heartfelt commitment, with potent, if incalculable, rewards.

Adam and Eve remind us that human work is deeply connected with God the Creator. In a sense they are invited to continue God's work in the world. But because they have strained the relationship, they can no longer remain in the garden God gave them. The difficulty of toil enters the world, and with it all the complexity and contradiction we experience today as we consider what work means.

"OUR PARTICIPATION IN LABOR IS A TOOL IN GOD'S HAND BY WHICH WE ARE CREATED, BY WHICH WE HELP CREATE. WORK JOINS US TO THE SUBSTANCE OF CREATION. WORK GRACES US WITH DIGNITY. WORK JOINS US TO GOD."

— *Fr. Daniel Homan, O.S.B.*

# What Is Work?

Is work an onerous burden, the result of sin, or a blessing that limits the effects of sin? Is work, as the Benedictine tradition insists, essential to maintaining good balance in a human community, while remaining in touch with God?

Our Christian faith is incarnational. God became man so man might become God, to take what has fallen and raise it back up to its proper place in the love of God's creation. While God's work in Christ is complete, it has yet to be fully realized in us. The gospels urge us on toward this discovery, and St. Benedict provides us with a practical guide to reconnect with God's creation through not only our prayer, but through our work and lives together.

In his chapter in the *Rule* on the Artisans of the Monastery, St. Benedict recalls the words of Scripture beckoning us to be good stewards of God's grace "so that in all things God may be glorified" (1 Peter 4:11). This is the witness the monastic life—as a particular expression of the Christian life—provides to the world.

"By means of work the monk shares in the creative action of God," writes Trappist monk Augustine Roberts. "Moreover, when united to Christ, we can redeem the world by our work. We can re-consecrate it to God and thus prepare the new world that will exist after the final resurrection."

And yet, some jobs feel like punishment, a daily grind wearing us down. And some seem so "unholy" as to be irredeemable. Perhaps the worst thing about such work is that it can cause people to think that this is all they are suited for. We have come a very long way from the garden.

## Extraordinary in the Ordinary

Yet the garden is where I find hope. And this hope is not a vague, wishful feeling but a solidly grounded faith in the God-given powers of the imagination. By that I mean the ability to recognize that, as Jewish tradition teaches, "All work done in imitation of God has an inherent dignity." Work seen in this light, Edward Sellner has written, is not only a blessing but also "a call to continue what God has begun."

Whenever I have witnessed work made holy, it is because ordinary people have taken ordinary tasks and made them something special. What might have been just a job to pay the bills becomes in their hands a vocation, and even ministry. My father, the son and grandson of Methodist pastors, was a model in this regard: the business card for his New Orleans Jazz Band of Hawaii read, "Playing the Truth in Hawaii." His vocation was bringing people together with joyful, danceable music.

God has indeed blessed us with the imagination to connect in creative ways with other people and the world—to see, in the words of poets, earth crammed with heaven and eternity in an hour. But there is also a divine grace that finds us in the most unlikely places. Two of my favorite characters in the film *Love, Actually* are a young man and woman who meet on the set of a pornographic film. Despite considerable odds, they grow in true, chaste affection. Their work leads them to holiness, and makes them whole.

Christianity asks us to consider not only the way things are, but the way God wants them to be, and will make them to be when the world is created anew. We need to be continually reminded, as Gerard Manley Hopkins writes, "It is not only prayer that gives God glory but work. Smiting on an anvil, sawing a beam, whitewashing a wall, driving horses, sweeping, scouring. To lift up the hands in prayer gives God glory, but a man with a dung fork in his hand, a woman with a slop pail, give Him glory, too. He is so great that all things give Him glory if you mean they should."

Hopkins' stress on human intention is something our mother Eve could appreciate. You can put up with a pouty husband, and even the pain of childbirth, because you know you are doing your part in something greater, something holy. After a dozen years as a caregiver, struggling with frustration and impatience, I am still amazed how quickly the air clears when I remind myself that I am engaged in doing the most important thing I could be doing with my life. When I tell people that my most spiritual act during the last year of my husband's life was cleaning out his commode every morning, they think I am joking. But I'm not. I am a member of a religion whose God became incarnate as an infant born among animals in a stable.

## Love Made Visible

At its best the Christian and Benedictine perspective on work is thoroughly holistic. In our work we obey the great commandment, expressing our love of God, neighbor, and self. The monastic and Celtic spiritual traditions especially embody this wisdom. Edward Sellner notes that the desert monks made repetitive manual labor an essential part of their prayer, and the Celts, he writes, regarded work as "love made visible." They made prayers for tasks such as lighting the morning fire or milking a cow.

When in his *Rule* St. Benedict speaks of the tools of the monastery, he refers not only to items used in worship, but the housekeeping, farming, and kitchen implements. All are to be blessed before use and treated with care. All are holy.

But it is hard to hold onto this wisdom as we go about our daily chores. It is difficult to love those closest to us at the end of a long day, when, as the poet Kate Daniels writes of her family, "We have all come home to each other to be healed and hailed … and morally realigned. But we are tired, and we lash out in irritation, frustration, anger." She laments, "Try as I may—and I do—I have a hard time browning the ground turkey I'm planning to mix with canned spaghetti sauce for the glory of God. I know that God is here, but in the chaos and the noise, I can't seem to find him."

Eventually she realizes that her seeking God at such a time is not futile, for it is in her very drudgery that God wants to find her. It's not when we think we are most holy, dressed up for church, as it were, that we are most accessible to God, but when we're sweaty and in a cranky mood, helping an elderly parent with a diaper. God knows and accepts us as we are, and that's good news.

## Change, Stability, and Work as Love

We live in a time of exponential change. According to a video that aired recently for the executives of a major media corporation, the 10 jobs considered most promising for today's students did not exist six years ago, and by the time they are 35 years old, these workers will have been employed in 10 to 14 different jobs.

The task of making work holy will become more difficult in this environment; we will need much creativity to find meaning in our work, and remain connected to each other and the world God gave us. The monastic perspective on work is more relevant than ever. Benedict asks monks to be committed to both stability and change, and Benedictine communities attest that lives centered on prayer can be flexible enough to survive some 1,700 years of human history while holding fast to the essentials of faith. Benedictines also give significant witness, in a workaholic age, to the balance we need so that work does not become obsessive and oppressive.

When daily life is honored with prayer at sunrise, noon, and sunset, work is put into proper perspective. One is invited to view work as part of the creation of a God who, as G. K. Chesterton suggests, "is strong enough to exult in monotony. It is possible that God says every morning, 'Do it again' to the sun; and every evening, 'Do it again' to the moon. It may be that God makes every daisy separately, but has never gotten tired of making them."

A friend has a poster on her wall that reads: "Anyone can slay a dragon, but it takes real guts to wake up every day and love the world all over again." This is what God asked of himself on the first six days of the creation, working, declaring it good, and then setting it aside until morning.

It is what God asks of us as we rise to face another day of work. Holy work as love, for a holy world reconnecting with creation.

## Listening with the Ear of the Heart

1. *How can the work we do to support ourselves and our families become praise and prayer in God's sight? Does that seem impossible? Too much to ask?*

2. *How do you approach your workday? Is the work you do merely a job, or a vocation you have been called to? Does that distinction matter?*

3. *In what way does the work you do—paid or unpaid—contribute to the life of your community? In what way does it help you participate in the life, suffering, death, and resurrection of Jesus Christ?*

There was in the Cells
an old man called Apollo.
If someone came to find him
about doing a piece of work,
he would set out joyfully,
saying, "I am going to work
with Christ today,
for the salvation of my soul,
for that is the reward he gives."

— *Sayings of the Desert Fathers*

"THE PERSON WHO
DISTRIBUTES THE GOODS
OF THE MONASTERY
SHOULD NOT BE
PRONE TO GREED,
NOR BE WASTEFUL AND
EXTRAVAGANT
WITH THE GOODS
OF THE MONASTERY,
BUT SHOULD DO
EVERYTHING
WITH MODERATION
AND ACCORDING TO
THE ABBOT'S INSTRUCTIONS."

— *Rule of St. Benedict, Ch. 31:12 (adapted)*

# Living Simply:
## Embracing the Gift of Peace

***by Rev. Dr. Jane Tomaine***

When has the desire for living simply come to you? For me the wake-up call came 20 years ago when I returned home from a retreat. After living in a simple room for the weekend where the sole objects were bed, desk, chair, and lamp, I was *shocked* to really *see* for the first time the incredible excess in my home. Occupying every available space was chair, desk, table, cabinet (filled with stuff, of course), lamp, rug, book, and knick-knack.

It hit me then how simple surroundings foster peace and spiritual openness, while the glut of "stuff" becomes a spiritual distraction and a sign of greed.

In the following years I made some progress in simplifying my surroundings and possessions. But several years ago when I was asked to lead a retreat on simplicity, a deeper realization came: "What do I really know about *living* simply?" Reality pointed in the opposite direction. I was queen of clutter, purveyor of piles, person of panic, finger-drummer at red lights, and sprinter in an over-scheduled life. Anxious thoughts of the day's to-do list would jump into my prayer and darken my thoughts. Yet, acceptance of the unlikely call to lead the retreat led me into a deeper quest for living simply. It is to this pursuit that I invite you, with the wise and benevolent St. Benedict as our guide.

# Benedict's Way of Simplicity

What does the Benedictine life offer that is so compelling for our 21st century lives? It is a life centered on Christ—flowing from Christ with roots that go deep into the nourishing soil of the gospels. "Prefer nothing whatever to Christ," St. Benedict advises, and "let peace be your quest and aim."

Centering life on Christ and seeking this peace form the foundation of simplicity and frame five supporting practices that I draw from St. Benedict's Rule: **Moderation, Balance and Flexibility, Attending to the Present Moment, Generosity of Spirit, and Time with God.**

These practices guide our relationship with possessions, with God, and with others to form a framework for living simply.

"BENEDICTINE SPIRITUALITY ASKS US TO SPEND OUR TIME WELL AND TO BE CAREFUL THAT OUR WANTS ARE NOT CONFUSED WITH OUR NEEDS AND TO TREAT THE WORLD AND EVERYTHING IN IT AS SACRED... BENEDICTINE SPIRITUALITY CALLS US TO BE MINDFUL."

*— Joan Chittister, O.S.B.*

# Moderation

Jesus said, "Do not store up for yourselves treasures on earth, where moth and rust consume and where thieves break in and steal; but store up for yourselves treasure in heaven" (Matt. 6:19-20a).

St. Benedict is adamant about the dangers of private possessions, calling private ownership in the monastery a "most evil practice." He even notes with disbelief that his monks might hide private possessions in their beds! He knows that possessions can distract as well as cause jealousy and envy among those in his community. But he also believes that legitimate needs are to be met out of respect and to prevent grumbling so that the monk's focus is on God.

Most of us cannot and should not give up all our possessions, but we can follow the Benedictine alternative. There is a difference between needs and wants. When it comes to clothing, food, work, possessions, and speech, St. Benedict emphasizes moderation. In the chapter on the clothing and footwear, he instructs that clothing is to be adequate and appropriate but not excessive, regarding anything more than two complete garments as "superfluous" (check your closets now!). And if a new garment is received, the old is to be given to the poor.

Moderation is an important ingredient in living simply because excess can affect us spiritually. In *The Way of Simplicity*, Esther de Waal writes that the desire to possess "will fill up that inner void which keeps a person open to the experience of God. ... While material goods are to be accepted, they are also to be regarded with detachment."

"Stuff" clutters our minds and hearts, blocks our journey to God, and undermines the biblical mandate for justice. In her book, *Wisdom Distilled from the Daily*, Joan Chittister, O.S.B., writes, "We have to pare life down to its simplest base" to "learn the difference between needs and wants so that the needs of all can be supplied."

Moderation also is important in time management. Taking on too much blocks living simply. St. Benedict explains, "all things are to be done in moderation because of the fainthearted." All things are to be arranged so that "the strong have something to yearn for and the weak have nothing to run from."

Simplicity also involves having reasonable expectations of others and ourselves. St. Benedict makes sure that people who need help are given help, and even makes it possible to question a task that seems too hard. He also encourages moderation in speech, explaining that even good words are not to be said out of esteem for silence. Living simply asks us to listen more and talk less.

## Balance and Flexibility

There is an ordered pattern of daily prayer, work, study, rest, and meals in Benedictine life. Such a balance of activities promotes living simply because it encourages a healthy wholeness—all aspects of life are honored and developed.

St. Benedict varies the type of work, the amount and type of food, and the necessary clothing with the person, their capabilities, and the task at hand. He also varies the daily schedule according to the time of year. Living simply requires us to be flexible with others, with ourselves, and with the circumstances of our lives. Change and differences must be taken into account.

*How* we do what we do is as important as *what* we do. There are two extremes—sloppiness on one end, and perfectionism on the other. We perfectionists are never—or rarely—satisfied. St. Benedict says gifts are to be used, but only if they do not become a source of pride. Living simply means performing a task to the best of our abilities without letting it absorb us.

When we live simply, moderately, and honestly, our lives have a grace and unity that bring our thoughts and actions into harmony.

## Attending to the Present Moment

Another aspect of simplicity is living in the present moment—being attentive to the people and situations before us. This can be difficult because so many things pull us away from the "now." We can be immersed in past regrets and angers, distracted by worries for the future, or seeking escape from people and situations.

Two of the vows made by a member of a Benedictine community provide a pathway for living in the present moment. The vow of stability is a lifetime promise to remain in the community. The vow of obedience is a promise to seek and follow God's will. These two vows remind us to remain connected with others (stability) and to listen for what God is calling us to do through the many people and situations that we encounter each day (obedience). We can embrace the spirit of these vows to ground our own lives in the present moment.

Acceptance helps us to remain present and fully open to God's grace in the moment. In his chapter on obedience St. Benedict says that when a monastic is asked to do something, that person should "lay down whatever they have in hand, leaving it unfinished" and do what is asked of them. In his chapter on humility he encourages the monastic to embrace even a difficult task without "weakening or seeking escape." Accepting what is before us rather than seeking escape leads to simplicity.

## Generosity of Spirit

Benedict believes deeply in the importance of community and the sanctity of relationships. Simplicity in relationships asks for generosity of spirit, respect for others, honesty, and a heart focused on harmony. His instructions can be summed up with these words from the chapter on Tools for Good Works: "Your way of acting should be different from the world's way; the love of Christ must come before all else."

He gives us many ways to be a peacemaker: Admit your mistakes, compete with one another in showing respect, support one another's weaknesses of body and behavior, be forgiving, serve one another, and refrain from grumbling.

One of the greatest obstacles to living simply is a desire to bend people or situations to our liking. When I exercise my "control muscles," life gets complicated. The Benedictine way reminds me of the need for humility—God is God; I am *not* God. St. Benedict instructs a monk visiting another monastery to be "simply content" with what he finds. The monk is invited to make constructive observations but not to make excessive demands or to find fault.

Throughout the *Rule*, St. Benedict also cautions against grumbling or murmuring. When we grumble or murmur to others, or ourselves, we are not "simply content" with what we find, but desire instead to mold people and circumstances to our own choosing.

Generosity of spirit applies to our relationship to the earth as well. Benedictines have a long history of conservation and care for the earth, living respectfully and in harmony with creation. We can embrace this way of living simply by using resources moderately, recycling, and taking steps to care for our beautiful and life-giving earth.

## Time with God

Common prayer is the priority around which life in the monastery revolves. Even if a person is away from the monastery, Benedict instructs that they are to "perform the Work of God," the prayers at the appointed hours. "Listen readily to holy reading, and devote yourself often to prayer," he says in the chapter on Tools for Good Works. If we are to live the Benedictine life and embrace living simply, we simply *must* pray!

St. Benedict knows that it is only through God's help that we can truly learn to prefer Christ and seek peace. Scripture beckons us: "Come to him, a living stone" and "let yourselves be built into a spiritual house, to be a holy priesthood" (1 Peter 2:4-5). It is Christ who helps us build this spiritual house of living simply.

With our hearts preferring nothing but Christ and our minds set on peace, we will be open to the transforming touch of God that will guide us to living simply the Benedictine way.

## Listening with the Ear of the Heart

1. *In the Benedictine life, what is most important is central, what is necessary is provided, and whatever would distract or encumber is let go. Take an audit of your possessions. What do you really <u>need</u>? What could you let go? Take an audit of your heart—learn to distinguish between want and need. Focus on what is really important.*

2. *Reflect on your life in each of the areas of Moderation, Balance and Flexibility, Attending to the Present Moment, Generosity of Spirit, and Time with God. Begin by taking one area to deepen your practice of living simply. Then move on to other areas.*

3. *Which relationships in your life are stressful? Is control a factor? What might you do to live more simply within these relationships?*

"BECAUSE OF HER INNER FREEDOM,
GERTRUDE COULD NOT BEAR TO KEEP ANYTHING
THAT SHE DID NOT NEED.
IF SHE RECEIVED PRESENTS, SHE ALMOST ALWAYS
DISTRIBUTED THEM QUICKLY TO OTHERS,
WITH THIS DISTINCTION:
SHE FAVORED THE NEEDY; AND
DID NOT PREFER HER FRIENDS TO HER ENEMIES...
IN CLOTHES AND OTHER THINGS SHE USED,
SHE ALWAYS PREFERRED
WHAT WAS NECESSARY OR USEFUL
TO WHAT WAS UNUSUAL OR PLEASURABLE."

*— Gertrude the Great*
*The Herald of Divine Love*
*cited in* Essential Monastic Wisdom *by Hugh Feiss, O.S.B.*

"THE FAITHFUL MUST ENDURE
EVERYTHING, EVEN CONTRADICTION,
FOR THE LORD'S SAKE."

*— Rule of St. Benedict, Ch. 7:38*

# Searching for Balance:

## Finding Hope In The Face Of Contradiction

***by Sr. Joan Chittister, O.S.B.***

"I've gone to church all my life," the woman said. "I don't know why these things keep happening to me." Her shoulders sagged a bit. "I just don't know how much longer I can keep going on like this."

I could hear the sense of futility in her voice. What is there to say at such a time? It wasn't that her problems weren't real. It was just that they were so normal, so predictable, and, at the same time, so depressing.

The "things that kept happening to her" from one year to the next were, unfortunately, all too common in this day and age: a dip in the pension, the downsizing of the job, the problem in the marriage, the struggle with one of the children, the death in the family, the slowly debilitating effects of the family genetic pattern, the alienation from a beloved sister.

Predictable, of course. Who doesn't go through such things? But unbearable? It all depends. Why things happen to us, however religious we think ourselves, is one thing. But how we deal with them spiritually when they do happen is another. The problem, after all, has nothing to do with who we are. The problem is that life is life. It treats all of us the same way.

# From Contradiction to Hope

"THE VERY CONTRADICTIONS IN MY LIFE ARE IN SOME WAYS SIGNS OF GOD'S MERCY TO ME."

*— Thomas Merton*

Life—everybody's life—is an excursion from dark to light, from contradiction to hope, from one circumstance and stage to another, all of them meant to stretch us to the fullness of ourselves and to the real meaning of what it is to be fully alive.

As a result, it is the way we deal with the dark and difficult moments that makes all the difference in how they affect us in the long run. And that has more to do with what we think life is supposed to be about than it does with the specifics of the present moment. Life, in the end, is really about learning to live it deeply, coming to live it well, beginning to live it as a spiritual experience rather than as a perpetual burden or an eternal Disneyland. Life is what takes us, eventually, one step at a time, to God.

It's easy, of course, to keep a religious checklist and call that a religious life. It is far more difficult to become a spiritual person for whom life is more of an adventure in spiritual growth and wisdom rather than a series of setbacks and an endless list of woes. God does not create us to tease our appetites and test our endurance. God creates us to enable us to see the Face of God in every dimension of life. As St. Catherine of Siena put it, "All the way to heaven is heaven." It is, however, a matter of coming to see it that way.

# Ancient Monastic Wisdom

Hardly anyone I know these days looks for advice in hard times from *The Sayings of the Desert Monastics*. And that's a shame. This collection of wisdom stories from third to fifth-century Christian hermits in the Egyptian desert is a treasure trove of spiritual insights. Each anecdote comes out of a hard-won, lifelong struggle to determine what it takes to live an honest, simple, prayerful, and deep spiritual life in a world in which religion had become more a social nicety than an intensely personal or private choice. Religion, these monastics knew, was not simply a cordial custom or a civil formality. It was a deeply personal and life-changing commitment. But there was a problem in that.

By that time, Christianity had become the official religion of the empire. Gone now were the political persecutions of earlier times and with them the consciousness of choice which that kind of pressure and resistance produces. In its place came official recognition and with it the patina of spiritual life—a kind of church-going claim to spiritual development. Being Christian was not a risk anymore. It was, for many—if not for most—a mundane routine, a badge of moral membership.

The spiritual life in these early Christian centuries, in other words, had become more and more like ours. Being Christian no longer constituted a threat to life or property. There was no real danger, no public onus that came with growing up Christian. Now, instead of martyrdom, it demanded much more. It demanded a different way of being human, another way of being holy at the very core of a world steeped in secularism.

In this world of secularism and mediocrity, materialism and superficiality, competing forces and turbulent contradictions, the desert monastics told their disciples stories such as the following:

*A brother who was insulted by another came to Abba Sisoes and said to him: "I was hurt by my brother and I want to avenge myself." The old man tried to console him and said: "Don't do that, my child. Leave vengeance to God." But the disciple said: "I will not quit until I avenge myself." Then the old man said: "Let us pray, brother." And standing up, he prayed, "O God, we no longer need you to take care of us since we now avenge ourselves."Hearing these words, the brother fell at the feet of the old man and said,"Forgive me, Abba. I am not going to fight with my brother anymore."*

The spiritual life, Abba Sisoes implied, has to do with accepting the vagaries of life with the certainty of God's love and the hope of

God's deliverance—in whatever fashion and in whatever form that might take. It does not have anything to do with being able to save ourselves from what we wish would not happen. It has to do with being able to balance whatever may happen with keeping hope and faith in God's presence even when it is difficult to recognize.

## Ordinary Life Lived Extraordinarily Well

Life is a medley of contradictions, but those contradictions are not its destruction; they are its essence. Contradictions are the juice to be extracted from life. They are the challenges that stretch our souls to the full and our hearts to a new consciousness of God.

It is of the essence of life to grow our souls into God by finding God at the end of every struggle, in the midst of every disappointment, at the heart of every breathless effort, at the corner of every dark turn in the road. It is at those moments that God takes over and we relinquish the struggle in order to allow faith to do for us what nothing else can.

Two spiritual traditions are based in hope and depend on balance to carry us through all the contradictions of life. The first, obviously, is the tradition of the Desert Monastics who threw their lives on the mercy of God, lived on little, and gave everything they had to the pursuit of the one thing that mattered in life—the awareness of the presence of God.

The second tradition that continues to nourish hope and provide balance is the sixth-century *Rule* of St. Benedict. Still the spiritual lifeline for thousands of monks, nuns, and oblates around the world, the *Rule* is a model for those who know that ordinary life lived extraordinarily well is the raw material of holiness.

Benedict's guide to hope and balance, though it permeates the entire *Rule,* lies chiefly in his keystone chapter (seven) on the 12 degrees of humility. It is humility—the capacity to recognize our tentative, temporary, fragile, and yet strangely secure place in the universe— that makes us right with the world. It brings shape to a right relationship with God, a right relationship with our spiritual guides, a right relationship with ourselves and the world, and a right relationship with those around us.

## God Is with Us

There is one thing Benedict teaches us before all other possible insights about the spiritual life and that is this: God is with us. It is as simple as that. God does not need to be earned. God cannot be merited. God is not persuaded by human behavior to attend to us. God is not intent on ignoring us. "The divine presence is everywhere," St. Benedict tells us.

God is the very breath of our souls, the creative energy that gives us life and carries us through all our days. God, our hope, is the magnet that draws us and the spirit that carries us from dark to light through life. Our beginning and our end is God, our present hope and life eternal.

We come to rest in that assurance, St. Benedict says, by realizing that whatever happens to us in life—when things go wrong, when our plans go awry, when our future seems dashed and the present seems impossible—God's will for us is our welfare and not woe.

Along the way, God sends guides to light our path—spiritual mentors and models to lead us, taskmasters to train us, disciplines to curb us—so that, for those "who endure and not grow weary," growth from the trivial to the significant may be complete. Then, aware of our own limitations, honest in our sense of self, subdued in our demands of the world and simple in our needs, we lose the demons of exaggerated expectations. We are ready now to take life as it comes to us, unafraid and secure in the presence of God to lead us through it.

## Taking Life as It Comes

Secure in this knowledge, we can truly begin to see the gifts and needs of others. We learn to respect those around us. We come to realize that the community of life is more important to us than the things of life or the control of life or the petty little powers that we once thought were the ultimate achievements of life.

Humility makes it possible to bear contradiction. It enables us to go on learning, to go on growing, to go on becoming more and more the face of the gentle Jesus to those who themselves are seeking it from us.

At that point, whatever life brings we can bear with equanimity because we know that God—no matter who we are or what we've done—is with us. And so are God's people, in this life and life eternal. However unprepared we feel or inadequate we are, there is a cloud of witnesses in the tradition and wisdom figures in the community whose goodness and insight are meant to be paragons and pillars to uphold the good spirit within us.

On these things we rest our hope and stake our balance—the everlasting presence of God, openness to guidance, honesty of heart, the wisdom of others—whatever the trials, contradictions, losses, struggles, and pain we face.

Then, as Abba Sisoes said, we put God back in charge of our lives and all the contradictions in the world cannot dim our hope or topple our spiritual balance as life carries us beyond ourselves to the very heart of God.

## Listening with the Ear of the Heart

1. *What does humility have to do with being able to bear contradictions in life?*

2. *In the seventh chapter of his* Rule, *St. Benedict deals with five levels of humility: our relationship with God, our relationship with those who have some official role in our lives, our attitudes about ourselves, our attitudes toward the circumstances of our lives, and our attitudes and actions toward others. What does humility look like in each of these situations? What does it have to do with having hope and balance in the face of contradictions?*

3. *Find a saying or story from the Desert Monastics and explain to someone else what you think the underlying spiritual wisdom is in the story.*

"UPHOLD ME, O LORD,
ACCORDING TO YOUR PROMISE,
AND I SHALL LIVE.
AND DO NOT CONFOUND ME
IN MY EXPECTATION."

— *The Suscipe*
*(Benedictine profession verse*
*from Psalm 118, Rule of St. Benedict, Ch. 58:21)*

“LET ALL GUESTS ARRIVING AT THE MONASTERY
BE RECEIVED AS CHRIST HIMSELF.
LET DUE HONOR BE PAID TO ALL,
ESPECIALLY TO THOSE WHO ARE OF THE
HOUSEHOLD OF FAITH, STRANGERS, THE POOR, AND
TRAVELERS.”

— *Rule of St. Benedict, Ch. 53:1,2,15 (paraphrased)*

# Offering Hospitality:
## How To Receive Others As Christ

***by Fr. Meinrad Brune, O.S.B.***

A friend wrote to me and shared with me the hard, emotional, serious problem he was going through with his family. I spent time on my letter of reply, but did not think it was a great one. This friend wrote back immediately and said: "Thank you for such a touching letter. Your words are healing medicine to my injured soul. I read the letter over and over."

After reading this friend's letter, I began to believe that it is not the guest—this friend—who is most favored when hospitality is offered, but the one who receives the guest—in this case, me. In offering hospitality to my friend by correspondence, I received happiness by his letter. I was blessed in exercising hospitality.

There is something sacred about being invited into someone's home. There is something even more sacred about being invited into someone's heart. I was invited into this friend's heart. I experienced the mystery of Christ's presence in this friend, and it was priceless. This was hospitality in reverse. I thought I was giving comfort to someone, and he in turn gave comfort to me.

## Scriptural Roots of Hospitality

The roots of hospitality are found in Scripture. In the tradition of the Bible, hospitality is twofold: it is a work of mercy and also a witness of faith. We see this in the story of Abraham and Sarah (Genesis 18). Abraham offered a spontaneous invitation to three passing strangers. His hospitality was a work of mercy. The strangers were tired, thirsty, and hungry. Abraham and Sarah worked hard to provide a kind welcome to them. The hard work is seen in the details of the preparation of the dinner. He greets them, then runs to find Sarah, goes to the cattle pen and picks a fine animal to be eaten, and tells the servants to cook the meal. Abraham and Sara play their role to perfection, acting as if the strangers are doing them a favor by accepting their hospitality.

"THE VOCATION OF A CHRISTIAN IS TO BE ANNOYED, EMBARRASSED, EXHAUSTED, AND CHEATED PERHAPS, FOR THE SAKE OF CHRISTIAN HOSPITALITY."

— *Walter Sullivan, O.S.B.*

But Abraham and Sarah's hospitality was also a witness of faith. They generously opened their bounty to the three strangers. These strangers turned out to be messengers of God who came to announce that elderly Abraham and Sarah would finally have a son of their own about the same time the following year.

The author of the Letter to the Hebrews probably had this scene in mind when he encourages us: "Do not neglect to show hospitality to strangers, for thereby some have entertained angels unawares" (Hebrews 13:2).

In the New Testament we see that God comes as a stranger into this world and receives hospitality from Mary of Nazareth. In the story of the Annunciation, Mary gave beautiful hospitality to God by saying "yes" to the angel. Jesus, the son of God and the son of man, was born of the Virgin Mary. God, who offers hospitality to all peoples, is manifested in the life and work of Jesus. Mary's faith and our acceptance of faith in Jesus witness to God's hospitality.

## Benedictine Hospitality

The hospitality of Abraham, Sarah, and Mary are echoed in the *Rule* of St. Benedict, which says that every stranger should be received as if he or she is Christ. St. Benedict wants his monks to attend to the needs of guests and strangers. If they are hungry, the monks feed them. If they are lonely, the monks give them their attention. If they want to talk, the monks listen.

But most of all, the monks just let them be. The greatest act of hospitality is when guests and strangers can feel comfortable and be themselves without fear of judgment.

St. Benedict teaches that the presence of Christ is mysteriously revealed in guests and strangers. Those who make room for guests and strangers are recognizing the mystery of Christ in them. St. Benedict wants us to become aware of the guest's presence and then extend a warm welcome. We discover the presence of Christ in them and then we respond to Christ by serving them.

The presence of Christ in others is the gift of life. We are given the opportunity at this moment to receive that gift, and it is for us a healing, enabling, empowering, and renewing experience.

Hospitality involves an attitude of openness to others, a sharing of food, of home, of self. We are gracious in allowing others to share those things with us. Making others feel welcome is the essence of Benedictine hospitality. We listen with care, we forgive with gentleness, and we treat others as persons of value.

It is inspiring to read a note of a visitor who wrote: "Guests like to be a part of something special. Most guests have a deep sense of home here: a feeling that they fit; that everything in their souls, their hearts, in their psyche is blessed and healed and soothed and challenged."

## Ingredients of Hospitality

***Offer a cordial welcome and courtesy.*** We should make guests and strangers feel welcome and that we are glad to see them.

My parents loved to entertain. All guests were made to feel special. At Christmastime relatives and friends were invited for dinner. The good dishes, silverware, linens, water goblets, and flowers were on the table. The whole family was part of making the guests feel at home.

My parents had a wonderful gift of offering people courtesy. Courtesy is primarily interior, and the polite forms are the outward signs of inner graciousness. Courtesy glows from the eyes, gleams in the smile, throbs in the tones of "thank you", "if you please", and "we are happy you are here."

These are simple ways of offering courtesy. Hilarie Belloc expressed courtesy in his lovely poem which begins: "Of courtesy, it is much less than courage of heart or holiness, yet in my walks it seems to me that the grace of God is in courtesy."

***Simplicity is enough.*** Sometimes we may think that our home is not good enough and we are not the best of cooks. But look at Martha and Mary in their home at Bethany (Luke 10). They welcomed into their simple home the Son of God, who had no home of his own. We share what we have and we do it in a simple and pleasant manner. Rich food and drink are not necessary, but what we have, we give with a kind spirit.

***Kindness and thoughtfulness.*** Acts of kindness and thoughtfulness matter the most in the end. Some of us are more forthcoming, more generous by temperament, and find it easier to make guests and strangers feel at home than others do. But something much deeper is at stake. It is a love of Jesus Christ which sees his image in every soul and comes out to meet it.

Kindness acts charitably without requiring or expecting to be rewarded in return. St. Benedict was touched by the kindness of a priest who came to him to share his Easter dinner. The priest said to St. Benedict: "This is Easter Day!" St. Benedict replied: "I know it is Easter Day because I have been granted to see you!" Through kindness and thoughtfulness St. Benedict experienced the presence of the Risen Christ in this priest.

***Spend time with the guest and stranger.*** The story of Martha and Mary gives witness to this ingredient of hospitality as they invited Jesus to their home. Martha was busy with preparing the meal for Jesus while her sister Mary sat at the feet of Jesus and listened to what Jesus had to say. Listening and being attentive to our guests are so essential in offering hospitality.

Jesus understood that Martha was doing necessary work to get dinner on the table. He knew her preparations were needed, so he was not scolding her. However, something else was even more important, and without this one thing all the work and all the effort were useless.

Mary's way contained the most essential element. She was listening, she was present, and she was fully in touch with Jesus. The one necessity in welcoming others into our homes is being present to them—listening to what they have to say, as Mary does.

Jesus needed to be heard and understood. Mary did just that. Mary spent time with Jesus and made him feel at home.

## Being at Home with Ourselves

We can only offer genuine hospitality if we are truly at home with ourselves. We should think long and hard on the words that St. Benedict uses in Chapter 53 of his *Rule* on the reception of guests—words such as "stranger", "poor", "traveler", "someone of the household of the faith."

These words describe us all. We who are poor strangers and travelers in the household of faith must welcome the hospitality offered to us before we can offer it to others.

The strangers that we are need the courtesy of love. The poor that we are need the strength of prayer. The travelers that we are need kindness and thoughtfulness. The members of the household of the faith that we are need understanding and attention. We must not forget that we cannot welcome the strangers, travelers, the poor, or members of the household of faith in others or see Christ in them unless we first welcome them within our very selves—as God welcomes us.

Only Jesus Christ could dare us to claim our identity in the same way we offer hospitality to ourselves first and then to others. What we do in hospitality to ourselves is much less important in the divine scheme than how well we become who we are created to be: living, loving beings in whom the spark of divine life can be clearly seen.

We are living, loving beings privileged by the gift of divine life, won for us by Christ's Resurrection to claim his name as our own: It is "no longer I who live, but it is Christ who lives in me" (Galatians 2:20).

So, we must ask, is Christ found in us and is Christ seen in others?

## Listening with the Ear of the Heart

1. *How well am I attentive to the ingredients of hospitality in my daily life?*
2. *Do I build space into my everyday life to take care of the traveler, the stranger, the poor within myself so that I can be in touch with seeing Christ in myself and then in others?*
3. *Think of a meeting you've had with a stranger to whom you offered hospitality. Did it turn out to be a hosting of angels unaware or a hosting of a less pleasant visitor?*

A BROTHER CAME TO A HERMIT,
AND AS HE WAS TAKING HIS LEAVE,
HE SAID, "FORGIVE ME, ABBA,
FOR PREVENTING YOU
FROM KEEPING YOUR RULE."
THE HERMIT ANSWERED,
"MY RULE IS TO WELCOME YOU WITH
HOSPITALITY, AND TO SEND YOU
ON YOUR WAY IN PEACE."

— *The Desert Fathers*

# Fidelitas
## (Faithfulness)

"THE WORKSHOP WHERE WE ARE
TO TOIL FAITHFULLY AT ALL THESE TASKS
IS THE ENCLOSURE OF THE MONASTERY
AND STABILITY IN THE COMMUNITY."

— *Rule of St. Benedict, Ch. 4:78*

# Anchoring Your Life
## Stability in a Moving World

***By Fr. Joel Rippinger, O.S.B.***

Mark Twain's Huckleberry Finn realizes the quest for freedom, but he has no intention of sticking around.

"I reckon I got to light out for the Territory ahead of the rest," he says at the end of the classic American novel, "Because Aunt Sally, she's going to adopt and sivilize me, and I can't stand it. I been there before."

Huck's restlessness is understandable under the circumstances, but one wonders whether he'd be more inclined to stay put in today's society—where pervasive mobility, a dizzying array of choices, rapid change, and a penetrating sense of the ephemeral feed our ravenous discontent. At the very least, perhaps the desire to raft down the Mississippi might give way to finding a safe inlet to put down anchor.

Escape, however, is not the goal, but rather true growth that requires commitment and leads to interior freedom. As Trappist monk Michael Casey writes in his book *An Unexciting Life,* "Stability prevents us from running away from necessary development."

If there is one mark of my own monastic vocation that I have discovered to be a compelling witness in my ministry to others, it is this virtue of stability. As someone who was born and raised in a homogeneous Catholic family and faith community about two miles from the monastic community where I have lived for over 40 years, I look with a sense of gratitude at the identity I have acquired from this experience. It certainly has helped to shape my sense of belonging, as well as create a focus for an awareness of who I am as a monk.

In a wider perspective, I see stability as generating a type of monastic mindfulness for all of us—an awareness of who we are, where we have come from, and where we are going. Certainly the potential witness of a physically stable group of committed people is nowhere more powerful today than in an American and global society in which transience and transplanted roots are demographic givens.

## A Vow and Virtue

Stability's place in the monastic tradition is a value beyond questioning. We hear the familiar refrain throughout the sayings of the Desert Fathers (the first Christian hermits) in the third and fourth centuries: "Stay in your cell and your cell will set you free." Adhering to stability was the way in which the "noonday demon" of acedia (spiritual apathy or restlessness) was overcome.

"THE INNER MEANING OF THE VOW OF STABILITY IS THAT WE EMBRACE LIFE AS WE FIND IT, IN THIS COMMUNITY, WITH THIS WORK, WITH THESE PROBLEMS, WITH THESE SHORT-COMINGS."

— *Cardinal Basil Hume, O.S.B.*

It was also the virtue that for St. Benedict in his *Rule* later distinguished the cenobites, those monks living in one place under a rule and an abbot, from the gyrovagues, who were constantly wandering (1:2, 10). It was the perseverance in stability vowed by the novice (58:17). When a visiting monk would choose to remain in a community, Benedict spoke of how he needed to "bind himself to stability" (61:5).

In another place Benedict tells his monks that they are not to go out of the enclosure of the monastery for the well-being of their souls (66:7). It is a saying whose relevance should not be lost in a world that has more in common with the moral menace of the Goths surrounding Benedict's monastery at Monte Cassino in the sixth century than one might think.

Perhaps to reinforce this point, Benedict employs in another part of his *Rule* the image of the monastery as a spiritual workshop, where monks are to execute the spiritual craft and practice stability in community (4:78). For Benedict and the other monks of his time, if one was truly single-minded in seeking God, then your commitment had to be to *one place*—for it was in that place where you would discover the truth about yourself.

The 12th century Cistercian abbot William of St. Thierry draws out the inner meaning of this when he tells his followers that it is impossible for someone who has faithfully fixed his soul upon one thing to not perseveringly attach his body to one place. Indeed, Stephen Harding, one of the founders of the Cistercian Order, instructed that the epitaph for his tombstone should read: "He loved the *Rule* and the place." The inextricable connection between these two has not been lost on subsequent generations of monks.

## A Place to Abide

Stability also has something to do with the structured life that is so identified with monasteries. Throughout history the space and architecture of monasteries came to symbolize a center of focused life in the midst of social flux and currents of change. Monasteries were places that provided spiritual and social stability.

It is not simply a question of providing a place where someone feels safe and secure. It is about providing a place where one abides. In this respect, it doesn't hurt that most of our monasteries have within their walls a church where Christ himself abides in the tabernacle. The language used to describe this in monastic tradition is revealing. Several times in the *Rule* Benedict speaks of the *domus dei,* the house of God, to refer to the monastery itself (31:19; 53:22; 64:5). Obviously, one looks differently at the place where he or she dwells if it is situated on the same plane as the dwelling of the Lord himself.

My understanding of stability also has something to do with an investment made in the land and locale. Unlike some religious orders, Benedictines have always been entrusted with the gift of a particular space they call home. The stewardship that has accompanied this investment in land has an obvious link with the vow of stability.

Some years ago I was looking through archival photos of American Benedictine monasteries while researching a history of the Benedictines in the United States. To look at the bleak and barren landscapes of the pioneer foundations and their primitive buildings, one can appreciate the transformation that was brought about in a matter of generations by assiduously cared for grounds and buildings. Indeed, monasteries beautify their locale.

This is not done, however, by creating a generic monastic theme park, but by taking on the specific contours and character that both conform to the regional characteristics of the monastery's setting and impart a unique insignia of landmarks and symbols that are readily identifiable. Benedictine writer Joan Chittister puts it precisely: "It is not the locale that binds, but our connectedness to life around it."

## "The Kingdom of God Is Within You"

Exterior stability is a very effective means to bring about interior stability. Benedict, I am certain, perceived a very close connection between the question "Who am I?" and "Where am I?" It is well rendered in contemporary fashion by the late Cardinal Basil Hume, who when still abbot of his English monastic community of Ampleforth, wrote: "The inner meaning of the vow of stability is that we embrace life as we find it, in this community, with this work, with these problems, with these shortcomings, knowing that this, and not any other, is our way to God."

In this view, stability is not restricted to a matter of geography, but is placed in the broader perspective of a relationship among persons who commit themselves to share their common search for God. Such a search needs an environment that facilitates it, and in an American society so characterized by social mobility and dislocation, the monastery becomes a centering force that counteracts some of the migratory behaviors of the surrounding culture.

At the heart of stability is a deep connection to the age-old religious longing to live life out from a center and to resist the recurring temptation to head somewhere else. It is a longing evoked by the psalmist who wants to dwell in the courts of the Lord all the days of his life (Psalm 27, 84). Even Jesus, when sending out his disciples, warns them not to wander from house to house.

The wisdom of monastic tradition tells the adherent that if you cannot find God in this one place, you are not likely to find God anywhere else. A stable monastic setting can also help us better appreciate the Gospel imperative that the "Kingdom of God is within you," embodied in the ordinary ebb and flow of life with others.

That is not to say that time in the monastery is an automatic ticket to holiness. It is quite possible for community members—more so than ever in the age of the Internet—to remain within the confines of the monastery all their life and still be unstable, both physically and spiritually. Forms of interior wandering and mental mobility, of being swayed by the fashion of the moment, are commonplace corruptions of the spirit of stability.

## A Witness of Presence

Without intending to be glib about the challenge of stability, it draws much of its force from simply "showing up." A person's bodily presence at prayer each day speaks as deeply as any other action about the need and importance of stability.

Whether it is the infirmary set coming in with their walkers and wheelchairs and electric carts, or the people who have just breathlessly made it into the choir stalls from another activity, their presence becomes a powerful sign of the solidarity of hearts and voices. It is a solidarity reinforced at Lauds and Vespers each day when the monks pray for the absent members of the community. Much like the deceased, their presence is missed but they remain a part of the community all the same. "Showing up" when it is multiplied by generations has a cumulative positive effect upon the community.

The opposite of showing up is giving up. Within monastic life are the same challenges as those encountered in other commitments: the grind of the daily routine, discouragement over goals not achieved, thoughts about leaving or starting over somewhere else. To the enticing strains of such suggestions, stability offers a two-fold prescription: patience and perseverance.

In the penultimate chapter of the *Rule,* Benedict exhorts the brethren to support with the greatest patience one another's weaknesses of body and behavior (72:5). In a similar vein, the *Rule* presumes that those who are serious about being formed in a monastic setting are persevering in their resolve (7:36, 58:3). Perhaps what stability injects into the perspective of the seeker is the expectation that the inner life and the exterior place intersect in stability, so that whatever happens as a result will endure.

The heart of the witness value of the vow and virtue of stability is to offer a space where hope can be sustained. In a cultural landscape littered with broken promises and dashed hopes, stability offers a space and fixed point of reference where promises and hopes are revered and revived. As Jesus tells us, "for where your treasure is, there your heart will also be" (Matthew 6:21).

## Listening with the Ear of the Heart

1. *Do I have a space that I can call my spiritual center from which I am fed?*

2. *How much of my spiritual life suffers from dislocation, rapid change, and the lack of a stable structure?*

3. *Who are the people in my life who have served as models of stability?*

A HERMIT SAID,
"A TREE CANNOT BEAR FRUIT
IF IT IS OFTEN TRANSPLANTED.
SO IT IS WITH THE MONK."

— *The Desert Fathers*

"OBEDIENCE IS A BLESSING
TO BE SHOWN BY ALL,
NOT ONLY TO THE ABBOT BUT ALSO
TO ONE ANOTHER, SINCE WE KNOW
THAT IT IS BY THE WAY OF OBEDIENCE
THAT WE GO TO GOD."

— *Rule of St. Benedict, Ch. 71:1-2*

# Obedience as Relationship

## Listening, Love in Action

***By Br. Francis de Sales Wagner, O.S.B.***

Obedience is a tough word to swallow. Something inside us instinctively rebels against it. We don't want to be obedient; we want to be independent. Generally speaking, we don't like anyone else telling us what to do, especially those who do not have authority over us.

There is another way of looking at obedience, however, and love is the key to understanding it, as St. Benedict knew well.

"Obedience for St. Benedict is love in action," says Benedictine monk Cyprian Smith. "Love is not simply a warm glow in the heart. The essence of love is giving, and if we are going to give generously in all circumstances, then there will be times when that will go against our natural wishes and feelings. The essence of obedience is putting others before myself. This means that we obey everyone, not only those who are placed in authority over us."

What this means is that obedience is more about our relationship with God and with one another than it is about simply following commands.

A 1988 hit song by country music artist Tanya Tucker illustrates this well by using the analogy of a tree. The refrain of the song:
*Like a tree out in the back yard,*

*that never has been broken by the wind.*
*Our love will last forever,*
*if we're strong enough to bend.*

Listening to this song, I am reminded that when one plants a tree, it is often necessary to temporarily support it against the wind until the roots take hold. However, experts insist that a tree should not be staked for *too* long. A tree builds strength by moving with the wind. Little by little, this movement increases its resistance to the occasional storm. A tree staked too long won't move with the wind. Ironically, its rigidity becomes its weakness. It doesn't build up enough strength, so is more susceptible to storm damage later on.

A tree needs to be strong enough to *bend,* and it needs to bend to *become* strong.

Likewise, to become strong, we must bend, and this bending takes place in the love we express toward one another through our daily interactions. Lasting, loving relationships, Tanya Tucker says, occur when we're strong enough to bend like a well-cared-for tree. St. Benedict would agree!

"OBEDIENCE (OB-AUDIRE) IS RELATED TO LISTENING (AUDIRE). THE OBEDIENT PERSON LISTENS TO OTHERS TO DISCOVER WHAT IS TRUE AND WHAT IS GOOD AND WHAT SHOULD BE DONE."

— *Fr. Hugh Feiss, O.S.B.*

# Growth, Rootedness, Flexibility

Christians are called to lives of conversion—to be conformed to the image of Christ, who is the Tree of Life. The Benedictine way of life is one way to respond to this call, and the Benedictine vow of *conversatio*—or conversion of life—is the goal.

Our purpose is to grow—little by little, year by year—into Christ, our Tree of Life. This gradual transformation constitutes our conversion, and it is a lifelong process.

But if growing into the Tree of Life is our goal, the other two Benedictine vows—stability and obedience—are useful tools to plant and maintain it.

Stability, or rootedness, requires commitment—physical, emotional, intellectual, and spiritual. It means being faithful to the promise God has made to us—whatever our state or circumstances.

Obedience, or flexibility, is being strong enough to bend, and it is the central theme in the *Rule* of St. Benedict. "Obedience," says St. Benedict, "is a blessing to be shown by all, not only to the abbot but also to one another as brothers, since we know that it is by this way of obedience that we go to God."

Directly or indirectly, St. Benedict emphasizes obedience throughout the *Rule:* "No one is to follow his own heart's desire" (3); "The brothers should serve one another" (35); "Trusting in God's help, the monk must in love obey" (68).

As Christians, we are *all* called to obedience. It is demanding, yet necessary. It releases us from the confinement of self-will, and stretches us beyond our self-imposed limitations. Mutual obedience, in particular, helps us to discover God and ourselves more fully—to become more fully ourselves through our relationships with those around us.

Wonderful things can happen when we consider a different point of view than our own, attempt something difficult we've been asked to do but did not choose ourselves, or trust that a challenging situation or person has something to teach us. We gain deeper insight, accomplish and come to enjoy things we never would have imagined possible, and find true happiness by seeking what benefits others rather than ourselves. ☙

## Impelled by Love to Listen

But aren't our *own* desires for good sufficient?

Our desires may in fact be good, but they can also be disordered—misguided by what we *think* our motivation may be. This is a result of original sin. Recall that the sin of our first parents was to do their own will, good though it seemed.

"The heart of original sin," says Trappist monk Augustine Roberts, "is the propensity to do our own will in opposition to the will of God. We have the tendency—which is the fruit of sin—to judge as good whatever attracts our self-love." The remedy for this, obviously, is Christ, who was obedient unto death in seeking our interests and not his own. "Follow me," he says. "Love one another as I love you" (Mark 8:34, John 15:12). By calling us to himself through his own obedience in love, he restores our broken relationship with God.

Too often, though, we can view obedience as a one-way street. For the person in authority, it can be a way to control and manipulate. And for the one who obeys, it can be done grudgingly as a means to another end. In either case, it becomes functional rather than a way of seeking God's will.

However, true obedience, as Christ models for us, is not concerned with exterior compliance but with interior motivation.

"It is love that impels us," St. Benedict says in the *Rule*. "Compliance with what is commanded is not cringing or sluggish or half-hearted, but free from any grumbling or any reaction of unwillingness. Obedience must be given gladly, for God loves a cheerful giver."

On the part of the person with authority, St. Benedict offers a thorough job description of the abbot, stating that he also is not to seek his own interests: "Rather, he should keep in mind that he has undertaken the care of souls for whom he must give an account."

So, true obedience is mutual and impelled by love rather than fear or self-interest, whether there is an element of authority involved or not. What this means is that in bending our will to God's will, we must bend the ear of our hearts to God's voice all around us—whether it comes from a superior, co-worker, parishioner, neighbor, family member, or friend, as well as from prayer, Scripture, and the life of the Church.

In short, we must *listen*—to everyone and everything. The very first word of the *Rule* is "Listen." And the Latin root of the word "obedience" means "listen." So, to obey is to listen.

## The Hard Work of Obedience

It is difficult—if not impossible—to listen to God's will by ourselves. God's voice is mediated through others, no matter how imperfect they may be.

"As Benedict sees it," says Benedictine monk Columba Stewart, "total dependence on God rather than on one's own desires and preferences develops best in community. The hard work of obedience happens in relationships."

Obviously, this is quite difficult even under the best of circumstances. It's one thing to learn something from a trusted friend or mentor. It's quite another to practice mutual obedience or seek God's will in a situation that seems to be without any redeeming value. That is precisely where our self-will puts up the biggest fight.

I am reminded of a monk who was consistently annoyed with an older confrere. He mentioned it to his spiritual director, who then asked, "So, what can you learn from this?"

That's not what the young monk wanted to hear. He was hoping for sympathy, and was challenged instead. This is a good illustration of how our own desires and inclinations can obscure what God is trying to tell us—often through imperfect human beings. It is also a good illustration of how others can help us to hear the voice of God in a particular situation. When this monk—prompted by his spiritual director—listened in his heart to why the older confrere upset him so much, he discovered a great deal about his own motivations and shortcomings.

"All of us can be mediators of God's will for one another," says Benedictine nun Aquinata Böckmann. "And God often uses rather fragile instruments to do it."

## How Do We Obey?

Our culture's emphasis on self-expression, autonomy, and self-fulfillment makes mutual obedience difficult. We want to be strong, but we rarely want to bend. However, what St. Benedict shows us is the true path to self-fulfillment. His way points to the self-giving of Christ.

"In real life, every person who has loving relationships and solid working relationships obeys, says Lonni Collins Pratt and Fr. Daniel Homan, the authors of Benedict's Way. "As uneasy as we are with the word itself, obedience is the key to lasting and healthy relationships. But it only works when we love and serve mutually, without conditions. If we have learned to obey, we will do it when it is not easy, when it costs us something."

Often, we obey in very simple, practical ways. A parent obeys by going to work each day, perhaps to a job that is less than ideal, because his or her family depends on it.

A monk obeys by rising early each morning to join his brothers in offering praise to God.

A friend obeys when rare free time to spend on a project is interrupted by another's need to talk about a problem.

A spouse obeys by listening to constructive criticism offered by his or her partner.

A grandparent obeys by reading the same book to a small child for the tenth time.

A widow or widower obeys by trusting in God enough to turn loneliness into inspiration for others.

"In everyday life we encounter all kinds of situations which are a constraint upon our initiative and our freedom in carrying out our tasks," observes Cardinal Basil Hume. "Other people's plans, other people's arrangements, other people's ideas or—quite simply—other people, frustrate us in one way or another. This, I think, is what St. Benedict had in mind when he talked about being obedient to one another. He did not mean just taking orders from others: he meant, rather, accepting the limitations which others impose upon us by the very fact that they are others."

## Strong Enough To Bend

Love in action sprouts from this recognition of our interdependence and mutual responsibility for one another. A true understanding of obedience, rooted in a committed life of prayer, is having the strength to bend like a tree in the wind.

This is our call, and it is a foretaste of heaven—our hearts and voices swaying in harmony with the breeze of God's whisper, like the sturdy branches of a mature tree that will last forever.

# Listening with the Ear of the Heart

1. *What is my reaction when I am asked to do something, or become aware of something that should be done, that I don't particularly wish to do? Why is my reaction what it is?*

2. *Do I truly listen to God's voice all around me? Do I obey because I must, or because I love?*

3. *What are some practical ways I can bend a little in order to help make the relationships in my life stronger?*

FOUR MONKS CAME TO PAMBO.
ONE FASTED, ONE OWNED NOTHING,
THE THIRD WAS A MAN OF CHARITY,
AND THE FOURTH LIVED IN OBEDIENCE
TO OTHERS. PAMBO SAID,
"THE LATTER HAS GREATER VIRTUE.
THE OTHER THREE USE THEIR OWN WILLS
TO KEEP THEIR PROMISES, BUT THIS ONE ROOTS OUT
HIS SELF-WILL AND MAKES
HIMSELF THE SERVANT OF ANOTHER'S WILL.
PEOPLE LIKE THAT,
IF THEY PERSEVERE TILL DEATH,
ARE SAINTS."

— *The Desert Fathers*

"THE ABBOT MUST SHOW THE TOUGH ATTITUDE
OF THE MASTER AND THE LOVING AFFECTION
OF A FATHER. HE SHOULD ALWAYS BEAR IN MIND
WHAT HE IS; HE SHOULD BEAR IN MIND
WHAT HE IS CALLED; AND LET HIM REALIZE
THAT MORE IS DEMANDED OF HIM
TO WHOM MORE IS ENTRUSTED."

— *Rule of St. Benedict, Ch. 2*

# Family Matters: Using St. Benedict's Rule As A Guide

***by Fr. Dwight Longenecker***

I was a college student when I first met a follower of St. Benedict. It wasn't a monk or a nun. It was a woman named June—a retired botany professor with white hair and an impish smile who lived in a cabin in the woods. June hired me for the day to help her with some gardening tasks. There was something attractive about this elderly lady that I hadn't encountered before.

She had a depth of character and beauty that I could not quite define. She was educated, but it never showed. She was a woman of prayer, but she wasn't pious. She had a good sense of humor, but she was never vulgar or common, sarcastic or mean.

In time, I came to realize that June's unique qualities were due to her commitment as a Benedictine oblate. June followed the principles of the Benedictine life, bestowing calm and beautiful depth to her life.

While the principles of Benedictine life were first formulated for men and women who were members of religious communities, they also provide a basic framework of practical spirituality for all Christians in every age. What's more, these principles for a stable and mature Christian life are not only applicable for retired ladies living in a cabin in the woods. They also apply to the everyday hustle and bustle of suburban family life.

# Families in Crisis

What should we do when our family seems to be going in 15 different directions? How do we manage to discipline our children with love and yet also with firmness? What are the proper values in our busy, materialistic society? How can we pray together when we are exhausted from work and the demands of family life?

Although the ancient *Rule* of St. Benedict may have been written for monks, it offers a practical and profound rule of life for lay people in many walks of life. And it provides some surprising and down-to-earth answers to the questions raised above relating to family life. The Rule's gentle wisdom and profound understanding of human nature offer guidance for ordinary Christian living, and its principles for living together in community provide excellent direction for the "domestic church" of the Christian home. ☙

"THE ABBOT HOLDS THE PLACE OF CHRIST. SO, TOO, THE FATHER AND MOTHER SHOULD ACT WITH ALL SIMPLICITY AND WISDOM, THE FIRMNESS AND GENTLENESS OF CHRIST."

— *Columba Cary-Elwes, O.S.B.*

# The Abbot as Model for Parents

Benedict says the abbot is the father of the community. Indeed, the word abbot comes from the term "Abba" which Jesus himself uses in addressing his heavenly father. The abbot also speaks with authority. He may be an earthly father, but he speaks for the heavenly father.

If Benedict's abbot speaks with this fatherly authority, it is meant to rule the monastery with the heavenly father's compassion, self-sacrificial love, and service. Benedict's abbot therefore presents modern Christian parents with an excellent role model. While Benedict speaks of fathers, the same underlying principles apply to the task of being a mother, with the obvious differences of style and emphasis that exist between men and women.

Benedict's principles for discipline are always measured and loving. He writes that "disciplinary measures should be proportionate to the nature of the fault." His basic form of discipline is "excommunication," though this is not the formal excommunication traditionally associated with church discipline. It is a separation of the person from communal life for a time. So, in the Christian home, the child who has done wrong should be sent to his or her room, or excluded from a family event or made to sit still on a chair or a special "quiet place."

However, even isolation must be moderate and restrained. Benedict says his *Rule* outlines "nothing which is harsh or burdensome." When somebody is punished, the abbot "should carry out with the deepest concern his responsibility for the brethren who fall into sin." He is to send another brother to console the one being punished in order to win him back in love.

In every case the abbot is directed to deal with discipline in a careful and solemn manner. Always being aware of human weakness, "he must bear in mind that it is the care of sick souls he has undertaken, not a despotic rule over healthy ones." This pattern of compassionate parenting may sound very modern, but it fits well with St. Paul, who wrote, "Fathers, do not exasperate your children; instead, bring them up in the training and instruction of the Lord" (Ephesians 6:4).

The Christian parent, like Benedict's abbot, must be flexible and loving toward each individual child. He "must adapt and fit himself to all … one to be encouraged, another to be rebuked, another persuaded, each according to his own nature. He must show the tough attitude of the master, and also the loving affection of a father." In every detail, Benedict's abbot is mature and balanced, always aware that his is a great responsibility: "The abbot should always bear in mind what he is; and let him realize that more is demanded of him to whom more is entrusted."

# The Divine Is in the Details

Benedict's *Rule* goes into great detail about how 6th-Century Italian monks live. We learn about their footwear, their clothes, their eating and drinking habits, and how they should sleep. He advises how old men, children, the sick, and guests should be looked after: "All who arrive as guests should be welcomed as Christ." He also goes into great detail about the monks' religious duties, laying down which Psalms they should sing during their services in church eight times a day.

All these details are interesting to read, but it seems difficult to imagine how they apply to busy 21st-Century families. Beneath all the mundane *matters,* Benedict is making the point that the mundane matters. The ordinary, *daily* details of what we wear, what we eat, how we worship, and what we read are all connected to our Christian life. Benedict would agree that if Jesus Christ hasn't gotten into our daily lives, then he hasn't gotten into our lives at all.

Some people say that "the devil is in the details." Benedict thinks the divine is in the details. The details are important, but beneath them is a spirit of discretion and Christian dignity. For example, from the *Rule* we can draw conclusions that a Christian family should be well fed and clothed, with care and comfort, but not with vanity or greed.

Benedict also sees material things as sacred, so the principles of the *Rule* help us have proper respect for possessions and the natural world. Benedict wants the monastery to be a secure and welcoming place; so, too, the Christian home is to be a place where the whole family lives together in abundant simplicity and looks outward with warm generosity.

The *Rule* teaches us balance and moderation in a consumerist society. St. Benedict helps us to love all things according to their true value, and so teaches us to pay attention to the little things that make life beautiful, rich, and abundant. He reminds us that the small duties are important because "he who is not faithful in a small thing will not be faithful in a large matter."

For these reasons, modern Christian parents can look to the *Rule* of St. Benedict for a sane and balanced approach to life—an approach that applies today yet links them with a time-honored tradition.

## Work and Prayer

Too often, it seems, we separate our working life from our prayer life. God gets an hour on Sunday; the boss gets all the rest of our time. The fact of the matter is, we work too much and pray too little.

The Benedictine motto *ora et labora* (pray and work) is a reminder that for Benedict, work and prayer are fused into a whole life dedicated to God. The *Rule* integrates prayer and praise with the most mundane activities in the kitchen, in administration, or study.

Likewise in the Christian home, no task is too menial to be integrated with prayer. The drudgery of life and the demands of parenting can be transformed by the Benedictine spirit, which sees each job as an expression of a deeper life of prayer and worship. It is beautiful to weave little prayers into daily life—a prayer of protection before travel; a prayer of blessing before meals; a prayer of thanks after a fun event; and prayers at the beginning and ending of each day.

At the heart of Benedict's wisdom is the assumption that the Christian family is a community of prayer. He gives detailed liturgical instructions, but balancing all the rules, he speaks clearly about the need for prayer to be natural and from the heart: "Indeed we must grasp that it is not by using many words that we shall get our prayers answered, but by purity of heart."

The oratory is the prayer chapel of the monastery, and it should be kept free so "if a brother should have a mind to pray by himself, he will not be disturbed." For a Christian family, it makes sense to have a special place in the home dedicated to prayer time. Decorating the space with an icon or some candles and flowers will help foster a prayerful atmosphere.

Every family will be relieved to discover that Benedict disapproves of long prayers. Prayer is better short and sharp than lengthy and long-winded: "Prayer therefore should be short and pure."

## Living and Loving Together

The *Rule* of St. Benedict is a treasure chest of practical wisdom on living together and loving together. While Benedict's writings are not instantly accessible to everyone, his principles are. There are plenty of books about the Benedictine way which make the bridge from the *Rule* to ordinary life for the average Christian. Whatever a person's place in life, St. Benedict offers a "little rule for beginners."

These principles of the spiritual life he sets down do not raise us to the esoteric heights of mystical speculation. They put us down firmly in life—right where we are. Benedict believes we should bloom where we're planted. God is to be found here and now, not there and then.

God is found in the face of our husbands, wives, and children. He is found in the terrible moments of family life as well as the wonderful moments. Benedict helps us to cope with the reality of life just where we are, and that is why his wisdom remains as fresh today as it was the day it was written more than 1,500 years ago.

## Listening with the Ear of the Heart

1. *Read Chapter 2 of Benedict's* Rule *(it can be found online at* www.osb.org *if you don't have a copy). What sort of lessons and guidelines might Benedict's "Qualities of the Abbot" have for you as a parent or guardian? Take this text to prayer and meditate about how it may be applied to the life in your family.*

2. *Most families seem busier than they care to be. Amid all the hustle and bustle, what are some details in your family life that could benefit from more recognition of the divine?*

3. *Does your family make time for prayer? Why not? What might you do to make time?*

"STRIVE TO BE LOVED BY YOUR SONS
RATHER THAN FEARED.
IF YOU WISH TO BE LOVED, LOVE!
A SUPERIOR WHO LOVES FOSTERS VIRTUES
WITH GOOD AND FREQUENT EXHORTATIONS
AND NURTURES SPIRITUAL PROGRESS.
HE CORRECTS THE ERRING
NOT AS AN ANGRY JUDGE,
BUT AS A LOVING FATHER."

— *Ludovico Barbo*

"Let us get up then, at long last,
for the Scriptures rouse us when they say:
It is high time for us to arise from sleep.
Let us open our eyes
to the light that comes from God,
and our ears to the voice
from heaven that every day calls out
this charge: If you hear his voice today,
do not harden your hearts...
Run while you have the light of life,
that the darkness of death
may not overtake you."

*— Rule of St. Benedict, Prologue 8-10,13*

# Caring For Creation

## Our Connection and Responsibility to Earth

***By Sr. Macrina Wiederkehr, O.S.B.***

A shadowy morning arrives. In my hermitage I sit in semi-darkness listening to the sound of raindrops on the roof. They are like pre-dawn music even though they hide the full moon's descent into the west. Night is dying. A dark, mystical morning is arriving.

I am using Mary Oliver's poem *The Kingfisher* and Psalm 24 for my prayer. I resonate with the poet's voice as she proclaims: "This is the prettiest world—so long as you don't mind a little dying, how could there be a day in your whole life that doesn't have its splash of happiness?" She is referring to the hungry Kingfisher acquiring his meal for the day. We know, of course, that the "silver leaf" with which he rises out of the waters is a fish.

Her piercing words assist me in understanding that while there is a necessary dying that is part of life, there is an unnecessary dying that destroys life before its time. Will we subject our planet to premature death due to our lack of care?

Words from Psalm 24 seep into my heart like the raindrops: "The earth is the Lord's and all it holds, the world and those who live there" (Psalm 24:1). Praying these words, I feel included, reverently held in the hands of God. The creation story from the book of Genesis echoes in my soul as I recall that "God looked at everything he had made, and he found it very good."

The glow from my candle lights up an artistic illustration of St. Benedict's vision as described in the *Dialogues of St. Gregory.* The prayer card I am beholding is a representation of the window in the Choir Chapel of Mount St. Scholastica in Atchison, Kansas. It is an image of Benedict kneeling in prayer holding the world in his hands. The light from this heavenly vision streams down on him, through him and onto the world. The world is aflame with the light of God.

I am deeply moved by the reality that, in Benedict's vision, the world is so small in the light of God's immensity, that the artist has Benedict holding it in his hands. As I continue to pray with Benedict's vision, a surprising lucidity overshadows me. I see it so clearly. Our vocation simply must include the noble work of listening to the cries of Earth. It is time to be attentive to the "deifying light that comes from God." We must put forth our very best efforts to assist in the healing of the Earth.

"WE NEED A SENSE OF BALANCE, OF ENOUGHNESS, OF STEWARDSHIP, AND A SENSE OF THE ETERNAL PRESENCE OF GOD. WE NEED A LIFE LIVED IN HARMONY WITH THE SEASONS… A COMMITMENT TO THE RHYTHM OF THE EARTH, THE NEEDS OF THE COMMUNITY, AND THE GOD OF CREATION."

— *Joan Chittister, O.S.B.*

## Unity of God's Creation

Reverence for the unity of life courses throughout St. Benedict's *Rule* for monks, though it is not explicitly stated. "We believe that the divine presence is everywhere," he says while outlining the proper disposition for the daily round of prayer. At another point, he stresses that one should "regard all utensils and goods of the monastery as sacred vessels of the altar, aware that nothing is to be neglected."

*Nothing is to be neglected*—neither prayer nor work, time nor matter. God's grace is intended to embrace the whole of life. With the sin of our parents, humanity broke off that embrace, but God beckons us back. The "good news" of the Gospel, fulfilled in Christ, seeks to restore the unity of God's Creation.

The monastic way of life is one way to live this call to turn back into the arms of God, to be restored in the image of our Creator. This includes our connection and responsibility to creation. Although St. Benedict's *Rule* does not issue a passionate summons for us to be caretakers of the Earth, if we are willing to dwell in the spaces between the words of his teachings, that responsibility becomes apparent.

## Reverence and Rhythm

St. Benedict implores us at the beginning of the *Rule* to listen with the ear of our heart. Today as we listen to the cries of Earth, how shall we respond? In countless ways the *Rule* calls us to live as people awake and aware, mindful and fully conscious, humble and grateful. We are to guard ourselves from avarice and anticipate the needs of others. We are to live in simplicity and moderation. Benedict advises against personal gratification. We must discern the difference between wants and needs, being grateful if we need less, humble if we need more.

The *Rule* is encircled with the call to reverence: reverence for the provisions of the monastery, reverence for the elders and the young, for the sick, for guests, reverence at prayer and for one another's need for silence. This spirit of reverence overflows into mindful living and becomes *time made holy.*

Benedictines have always tried to be obedient to rhythms of light and darkness created by the Earth's turning. We are attentive to the hours of the day and the seasons. Hopefully, those with Benedictine hearts will hear a call to honor the Earth with the same spirit of reverence.

## Sustaining the Necessary

*Sustain me by your promise that I may live;*
*do not disappoint me in my hope.*
**(Psalm 119:116)**

This verse, the *Suscipe* we sing at our monastic profession, is our total self-gift to God, to one another, and to the world. It is our way of saying, "receive me, sustain me, uphold me. Do with me whatever is necessary for the good of the entire earth family."

In order to sustain ourselves and be sustained by God's promise, we make every effort to supply all that is necessary for healthy community living. We support, care for, and encourage one another, especially in the face of burdens or danger. "Bear one another's burdens" (Galatians 6:2). We assist one another to endure in the face of discouraging circumstances. We search for ways to contribute to the good of the community. We uphold one another.

As we reverentially uphold one another in community, we must extend the call "to sustain" out to the cradled world of Benedict's vision—that world bathed in heaven's light. Perhaps it is not outside our reach, if we simply open our eyes to see the connection between our individual community's need to be sustained and the larger world community that needs our support and upholding.

The word *sustainability* is often used today in reference to ways to sustain the Earth, to keep it livable and healthy for future generations. Our total self-gift to God and community must extend beyond the immediate community and give shape to our own relationship with the Earth.

Since their founding, Benedictines have created small, sustainable, and self-sufficient societies in which members, by the labor of their hands, live simply and communally. Benedictines have always placed emphasis on what is needed rather than wanted.

Benedict's vision of the Earth bathed in the light of God must become our own vision. As we pray, "The earth is the Lord's and all it holds..." let us strive to remember that it holds us all, burdened and blessed in so many ways. We who have publicly proclaimed the gift of ourselves as eager to meet these needs must take all this to heart, and examine our consciousness of creation.

# Earth Consciousness Examination

How well do I offer hospitality to the Earth? How aware am I of the depletion of the Earth's natural resources and my part in it? Am I willing to expand my awareness in the area of Earth stewardship?

How often do I recycle and reuse? If I do not recycle, what is my underlying reason for not doing so? Have I considered purchasing locally when possible? Am I willing to carpool and conserve trips? When I refuse to carpool, what is the principle reason for not doing so? When possible, would I be willing to use public transportation?

Am I aware that I can save energy by unplugging electrical appliances when not in use? Would I consider making this part of my everyday life? Am I willing to educate myself on how I may be contributing to some of the harmful toxins in my environment? Do I make every effort possible to use non-aerosol products?

How aware am I of over-consumption in any of these areas? Am I conscious of the impending water crisis and what this means for our future? Do I take time to enjoy the beauty of the Earth?

One reason why trying to be good stewards of Earth is so overwhelming for many of us is that the changes we make in our lifestyle do not seem to bring about any observable changes in the environment. Because the results are not immediately noticeable, it is easy to assume that our efforts are fruitless or futile. Clearly though, how we live on Earth collectively makes a difference; one only needs to look at the evidence neglect has provided.

# The Book of Creation

When I was a novice, the benches on our monastery grounds were frequently occupied with sisters relaxing in prayer, reading, enjoying the book of creation, or doing their *lectio divina* (sacred reading) in the beautiful outdoors.

Today this is not the case, and I do not believe it is just because we are older now. Some of the busyness of our society has crept into our monastic living, and we often choose to sit in front of our computers rather than on park benches.

I dream of the day we will do *lectio* on, and with, creation again. As can be seen in this little story from the Desert Fathers, creation has often been called the first book of Scripture:

> *One day, a Greek philosopher journeyed to visit Abba Anthony. Upon entering his cell, the philosopher was shocked to find it empty of books. "How can you be so happy, when you do not have the comfort of books?" the philosopher exclaimed. Anthony looked out over the vast desert and replied, "My book, O philosopher, is the nature of created things, and as often as I have a mind to read the words of God, it is in my hands."*

## The Path of Prayer

Perhaps our sensitivity to the cries of Earth would amplify if we could find our way to a greater faithfulness in praying creation.

A few years ago about 25 retreatants and friends of our Retreat Center created a labyrinth on our grounds. The path is lined with creek stones. Wood chips and pine needles serve as ground for the path. Walking this sacred trail offers both guests and community members a new opportunity to listen to the Earth and pray creation.

As you pray, look around you at God's creation. Listen to it. What is it saying to *you*? Can you see Benedict's vision of the Earth bathed in the light of God? What sort of path can you build to turn back into the embrace of our Creator?

## Listening with the Ear of the Heart

*O Holy Father Benedict, implore the God of your vision, the God of Light, to shine once again upon this planet, so broken and beautiful, fragile, and fruitful. Transform us into prophets. Increase our love for the Earth that serves us so faithfully. Inspire us to be a vital part in the mending of this planet. Open our ears to the cries of Earth. May it come to pass.*

While Benedict was keeping his vigil
... he suddenly looked and saw that
a light, shed from above,
had scattered all the shades of night.
... The whole world,
as though gathered up
under a single ray of the sun,
was brought before his eyes.
To a soul that beholds the Creator,
all creation is narrow in compass.
For when we view the Creator's light,
no matter how little of it,
all creation becomes small in our eyes.
By the light of the inmost vision,
the inner recesses of the mind
are opened up and so expanded in God
that they are above the universe.

— *Dialogues of St. Gregory*

# Conversatio
## (Conversion)

"AS WE PROGRESS IN THE MONASTIC LIFE
AND IN FAITH, OUR HEARTS WILL SWELL
WITH THE UNSPEAKABLE
SWEETNESS OF LOVE ENABLING US
TO RACE ALONG THE WAY OF
GOD'S COMMANDMENTS."

*— Rule of St. Benedict, Prologue, 49*

# Our Call to Conversion

## Growing in Our Relationship With God

***by Sr. Laura Swan, O.S.B.***

In the movie *As Good As It Gets,* Jack Nicholson's rude and obnoxious character, Melvin Udall, is about to blow it with the woman he's fallen in love with. He wants to pay Carol Connelly (Helen Hunt) a compliment, but can't seem to find the words in his typically self-absorbed and insulting vocabulary.

Suddenly, a glimmer of light pierces the darkness:

"You make me want to be a better man," he tells her.

He is sincere, and it shows in his efforts—albeit still stumbling and bumbling at times—to step out of his shell and into the lives of others.

*Falling in love* is risky business. We are pulled out of ourselves and into the life of the one we love. It is both exhilarating and disorienting. Our sense of direction shifts—how we spend our time and energy. Our perceptions of life expand and refocus.

Friends and family notice that, somehow, we are "different." We hear in new ways. We notice things we hadn't noticed before. Our beloved begins shaping how we relate to the world: our taste in music and books and art may broaden; we meet new friends; and we take on new responsibilities.

Falling in love *changes* us. And yet in so many ways, it heightens the truth of who we authentically are. We become more ourselves.

This is conversion.

# A New Way of Relating

"Conversion is powered by hope: life is an ever-flowing stream and it is never too late to find the deep current. Sometimes it may be necessary to float for a while. Walking on water is optional."

— *Sr. Mary Giles Mailhot, O.S.B.*

Perhaps the fictional life of Melvin Udall is not the *best* illustration of conversion in the Christian tradition. However, in our faith, when we pray in all sincerity and truth, we are saying to God, "You make me want to be a better person. Show me; help me." And this desire is borne of a love that comes from sheer grace. The God whom we seek to give ourselves is both the means and the end.

This conversion is a commitment to further growth rooted in the love we have for God. It is not a moment, but rather a lifetime—which includes some occasional stumbling along the way with all the Melvin Udalls of the world.

"Conversion is a falling in love with God—not as a one-time event, but as an ever-deepening relationship," says Fr. Mark O'Keefe, O.S.B., a monk of Saint Meinrad Archabbey. "Prayer is the language of this conversion."

This language of love invites us to new ways of relating with God, our neighbors, and ourselves.

This invitation is for everyone. Benedictine monks and nuns—who take vows of conversion of life, stability, and obedience—live out the call to conversion of life through prayer in a very specific and explicit way. However, it is the primary work of anyone truly dedicated to the Gospel.

When St. Benedict speaks of conversion in his *Rule,* "he is talking about a change of direction in our lives, a pursuit of goals different from those we have pursued hitherto," says Cyprian Smith, O.S.B., in *The Path of Life*. "When a monk takes this vow, he is promising to change his way of life; from now on, both his inner attitude and his outward behavior are going to be different from what is regarded as normal in the world." And "all Christians, not monks alone, are called to recognize that there is more to life than the pursuit of worldly ends."

But there is still more. While conversion involves turning around, changing, and moving away from sin and toward righteousness, God wants so much more than that. While it is important that we seek to transform serious character defects, that we end harmful behaviors and mend broken relationships—traditionally called sin—and that we give our assent to transformation through the power of the Holy Spirit, conversion involves transformation of attitudes and motives and perspectives.

Conversion is about discovering and growing in our relationship with God, about maturing in our relationship with the Source of Life, Unconditional Love and Fount of Wisdom. This involves a commitment to total, absolute, unconditional, whole-hearted surrender of self, along with the knowledge that this is a lifelong process and not an overnight success.

Commitment is the key. While new relationships enrich and broaden our lives, they also require work, time, and tender care. Relationships are meant to grow and deepen and mature. As we must give in order to receive, we must honestly communicate with each other. Otherwise the relationship may grow stagnant and stale, dry and boring, and risks dying.

As with our human relationships, so it is with our Creator.

Each day of this new loving relationship with God, we are invited to discover a new part of ourselves that we had not known existed before. New strengths emerge as we build and protect and nurture this new way of relating with God, our neighbors, and ourselves.

Hopefully, each new day we become a new person, more closely resembling our Creator and Redeemer.

# Listen!

St. Benedict was handed a motley crew of beginners to the monastic way of life and sought to shape them into saints. He perceived possibility in his new converts—an odd mixture of men his society would declare could never serve the Gospel, let alone live peaceably with each other!

St. Benedict accepted members of the elite patrician class and slaves; the illiterate and highly educated; and men whose clans were sworn enemies of each other. But Benedict knew, believing beyond all hope and worldly wisdom, that in following the small steps of his *little rule,* grounded in the Good News of Jesus, these men would slowly transform into the image and likeness of Christ.

Why? Because they were all motivated by love for God and desire for a deep and intimate relationship with God.

And so St. Benedict began his *Rule* with *"Obsculta,"* or "Listen." We pay attention, listen and receive; we listen and are taught.

"Listen to the silence and the silence will teach you everything," the desert ascetics tell us. Listening is the beginning of all wisdom. In listening with the ear of our heart we are open to having our deeply held convictions and opinions challenged; we are willing to consider other possibilities and perspectives; we are willing to change.

St. Benedict taught that listening is the stance toward life that builds, nurtures, and transforms relationships. Listening is the posture of the disciple toward the venerable teacher.

In his *Rule,* Benedict exhorts: "Let us get up then at long last, for the scriptures rouse us when they say, 'It is high time for us to arise from sleep.' Let us open our eyes to the light that comes from God, and our ears to the voice from the heavens that every day calls out this charge: 'If you hear God's voice today, do not harden your hearts.' And again: 'You that have ears to hear, listen to what the Spirit says to the churches.' And what does the Spirit say? 'Come and listen to me: I will teach you to reverence God.' "

# Self-Awareness

Relationships teach us something about who we are and what we value. Conversion is that day-to-day faithfulness to matters small and large, through excruciatingly painful times and joyous times that build character. Conversion deepens our self-awareness, of who we are and how we are before God.

Self-awareness is that capacity to recognize how the Holy One chooses to relate to us, in friendship and intimacy. Sometimes we do not like what we see, and a path toward change and transformation opens up before us.

To the extent that we know ourselves, we know God. God has chosen this for us, that as we grow in self-knowledge and self-awareness, we become more alert to *how* God chooses to connect with us, and journey with us through life.

But like any relationship, we must continue to work at it, day after day. We cannot become complacent or remain interiorly dead. If our inner world dies, so too does the relationship.

# Freedom and Compassion

Conversion is a movement toward interior freedom. The spiritual journey is not about "should" and "ought," but rather about the desire to be attentive, to be friends with God and one another, to be willing and joy-filled companions.

Mature relationships are built on trust. As we mature in our relationship with God and one another, we are open and willing to learn from life.

Our call is fidelity to the spiritual journey: through hard times and joyous times; when others hurt us and surprise us with their compassionate support. In fidelity, we exercise staying power. We do not run from discomfort or pain; rather, we face into the situation, seeking God's will. Life's challenging experiences foster compassion within; when we see others struggling, we more easily empathize.

This cultivates holiness—the balanced wholeness for which Benedict's *Rule* is so famous. Thus, with the writer of First Peter, we commit: "As God who called you is holy, be holy yourselves in all your conduct; for it is written, 'You shall be holy, for I am holy' " (1 Peter 1:15-16).

This can be quite difficult—sometimes agonizingly difficult. Yet in trust and the staying vision of stability, we are changed and our difficult situations are transformed. Along the way, God's Word is there to encourage us: "Trust in the Lord … Commit your way to the Lord … Be still before the Lord; wait patiently … Our steps are made firm by the Lord" (Psalm 37:3, 5, 7, 23).

Conversion is a daily commitment to stay the journey, remaining true to the course given us, trusting the process that we will become the people we were created to be and to serve God as we were meant. "What is more delightful than this voice of the Holy One calling to us?" St. Benedict asks. "See how God's love shows us the way of life. Clothed, then, with faith and the performance of good works, let us set out on this way, with the Gospel for our guide, that we may deserve to see the Holy One, who has called us to the eternal presence."

Let loving desire be your motivation to become a better person. Set about doing the things you need to do to deepen and broaden, and to stretch beyond all imaginable heights and breadths and depths.

As modern mystic Evelyn Underhill said: "God is not so much interested in nibblers of the possible but grabbers of the impossible." Falling in Love allows us to do this. God is Love, and as Virgil said, "Love conquers all."

## Listening with the Ear of the Heart

*God, source of all wisdom and our ever-sustaining hope, you yearn that we, your people, would draw ever close to you. You entice us toward intimacy and friendship.*

*Breathe into our hearts a yearning for divine union with you. Deepen our awareness of our hunger for you. And bring forth healing and transformation.*

*We ask this, now and always. Amen*

"Where the Spirit of our Lord
is working in a soul
there is, and must be,
Liberty and no restraint,
whereby the Spirit may work freely.
In interior simplicity the Spirit
is in perfect Liberty
and able to journey
toward God in wholeness."

*— Dame Gertrude More, O.S.B.*

"THE ABBOT SHOULD BE DISCERNING
AND MODERATE, BEARING IN MIND
THE DISCRETION OF HOLY JACOB,
WHO SAID: 'IF I DRIVE MY FLOCKS TOO HARD,
THEY WILL ALL DIE IN A SINGLE DAY.'
DRAWING ON THIS
AND OTHER EXAMPLES OF DISCRETION,
THE MOTHER OF VIRTUES,
HE MUST SO ARRANGE EVERYTHING
THAT THE STRONG HAVE SOMETHING
TO YEARN FOR AND THE WEAK
NOTHING TO RUN FROM."

— *Rule of St. Benedict, Ch. 64:17-19*

# Conceiving Virtue
## Temperance, Discretion, Humility, and Love in the Monastic Tradition

***by Fr. Harry Hagan, O.S.B.***

St. Benedict in his *Rule* calls discretion the "mother of virtue" (64:19), following a tradition of many others who chose various virtues as the mother of *all* virtues. Cicero, one of the earliest, chose gratitude, and others named justice, obedience, and patience.

However, early Christian writers focused mainly on four chief virtues: temperance, discretion, humility, and love. While temperance and discretion have their roots in the world of Greek philosophy, humility and love take their understanding from the Christian gospel.

## Temperance as the Mother of Virtue

Plato proposes in *The Republic* four cardinal virtues: prudence, courage, temperance, and justice. The Greek *sōphrosynē*, translated "temperance" or "self-restraint," refers primarily to a matter of self-control that allows people to exercise what they judge to be virtuous. Aristotle also makes temperance the basis for the virtuous life because he understands virtue as the mean between too much and too little. This idea is captured in the Latin saying *in media stat virtus*— "in the middle stands virtue." Temperance allows a person to hold to the middle, so it is not surprising that some call temperance, or some version of it, the mother of virtue.

However, recognizing the middle brings its own problems because the middle is not always in the middle. Depending on the particular situation, sometimes more or less is needed to find the proper balance. Plato and Aristotle called the ability to discern this prudence or wisdom. The Greek word suggests "a practical understanding or wisdom" that allows a person to handle the situations of life by deciding where the middle lies. In the monastic tradition, the ability is referred to as *anakrisis,* which means judgment or discretion—the judgment about where the middle lies. A person with prudence can recognize what one must do to stand in the middle, and so be virtuous.

"ST. BENEDICT WAS A WISE ABBOT. HE WAS FLEXIBLE AND MODERATE. HEROIC VIRTUE IS NOT DEMANDED."

— *Br. Benet Tvedten, O.S.B.*

In the monastic tradition, self-control goes beyond temperance and becomes *askēsis*—the Greek word meaning "exercise and training." The Christian ascetics, in their search for total purification and full union with God, look down on lukewarm solutions. This kind of zeal, however, easily allows distortion, as early monk and writer John Cassian recognizes.

## Discretion as the Mother of Virtue

Cassian and his friend Germanus left their monastery in Palestine for the Egyptian desert—the vibrant center of monastic life in the 4th Century. There, the two young monks sought out the great abbas, or spiritual fathers, to hear their conferences on monastic life. In 400 A.D., a theological backlash against the followers of Origen forced John Cassian to flee Egypt. After stays in Constantinople and Rome, he founded a monastery in Marseille and wrote two fundamental books on monasticism based on his experience in Egypt. *The Institutes* describe the ways of the monk and dealing with the eight passions. In *The Conferences*, Cassian recounts 24 lectures which he and Germanus supposedly heard in the desert.

Abba Moses gives the first two conferences, and he tells Cassian and Germanus: "I want to tell you a little more about the sublimity and grace of *discretio*, which among all virtues holds the supreme and first place…" He goes on to call discretion "that virtue which is the mother (*genetrix*) of moderation." Abba Moses begins his explanation with a story about the elders of the desert gathering one night to discuss which virtue is able preserve a monk from the snares of the devil. Some name zeal in fasting and vigils, some choose the despising of material things, some believe that the withdrawal from the world is essential, and still others insist on the duties of charity. Finally, Abba Anthony the Great declares that only discretion is able to protect a monk from both the excess of asceticism and from the slackness that leads to vice.

Abba Moses tells the story of the old monk Heron, who maintained a fast with such extraordinary strictness that he would not even break it for the celebration of Easter: "Deceived by this presumption, he welcomed with the highest veneration the angel of Satan as an angel of light," who told him that he was so holy that he could not hurt himself even if he threw himself down a well. Deluded by his pride, Heron threw himself down the well. Discretion, then, is the ability to judge where the middle can be found to avoid extremes. As a result, Abba Moses calls discretion "the mother, guardian, and moderator of all virtues."

Benedict follows Cassian in making discretion the mother of virtue. However, this idea of balance and practical wisdom pervades Benedict's *Rule* to a greater degree than it does in Cassian's writings. Benedict's great chapter on discretion is 64, in which he makes the abbot the great example of discretion. Early in the chapter, Benedict touches on the theme of wisdom by calling for the community to choose an abbot for his "goodness of life and wisdom in teaching."

The word "prudence" appears twice. When punishing the brothers, the abbot "should act prudently and not overdo it" lest he break the pot by rubbing too hard or crush the bruised reed. Moreover he should "not permit vices to flourish but he ... should prune them with prudence and charity…best suited to the individual."

"The abbot should be farsighted and thoughtful" and in his orders "should be discerning and moderate." "To discern" is the verb form of discretion, and this judgment allows a person to be moderate. As a result, the abbot should bear "in mind the discretion of holy Jacob who said: 'If I make my flock walk too far, they will all die in one day'" (Genesis 33:13). The abbot must not push too much. Still, he should "arrange everything so that the strong are challenged and the feeble are not overwhelmed."

Many have recognized the centrality of discretion to the spirit of St. Benedict. Still, when you begin to look beyond Chapter 64, the vocabulary seems at first to be missing. Yet, the word "measure" appears 15 times and provides the most pervasive concrete image of discretion—whether it be the measure of food, drink, clothes, or the measured arrangement of work. Decisions should be made with *consideration,* which is linked particularly to the consideration of the sick and the weak, to the very young and the very old.

In Chapter 63:5-6, Benedict indicates that age, which should bear the fruit of wisdom, is no guarantee of discretion, and he cites David and Daniel as youths who "judged the priests." The verb *judicare* ("to judge") appears three times with *utilis* meaning "useful, fit, profitable, serviceable" to capture the practical wisdom so valued by Plato and Aristotle. Though "wisdom" (*sapientia*) appears only twice, its adjective "wise" (*sapiens*) appears 10 times. In dealing with the excommunicated, the abbot is twice called to be "a wise physician." Likewise, the cellarer and the porter are to be chosen because they are wise. Benedict says in Chapter 53: "The house of God should be wisely managed by wise persons."

From a biblical perspective, wisdom is related to the "fear of the Lord," for "the fear of the Lord is the beginning of wisdom" (Psalm

111:10). Therefore the Prologue of the *Rule* calls out: "Come, children, hear me; I will teach you the fear of the Lord." The words for fear (*timere* and *timor*) appear 22 times in the *Rule*. Although there is a bad fear, the "fear of God" is always a good fear in the *Rule*, and Benedict requires this fear of God from many in the monastery: from the abbot, the obedient, those at the first step of humility, the cellarer, the infirmarian, the guest master, etc. This 'Who's Who' of the monastery demonstrates the importance of "the fear of the Lord," and its biblical base ties it to wisdom and therefore to discretion.

Benedict's discretion shows itself as well in his balanced approach to regulations. In the Prologue, he says that "the reason of fairness" may require "something a little more restrictive" but "nothing harsh, nothing oppressive," and then only "to correct vice or to preserve charity." If "a little" deals with the situation, then let "a little" be done. Moreover, the abbot should decide how much is enough—enough food or drink, enough bedding or clothing, etc. As in all things, the abbot is the guardian of the mean.

Benedict uses the Latin word *regula* to refer mainly to his written document, but more generally this word means "a rod used for drawing straight lines or measuring, a ruler." As such it belongs to the language of measure. However, Benedict realizes that his written document cannot always provide the definitive answer. So he gives the abbot freedom to change, modify, and interpret what has been written. Interestingly, the *Rule* also directs the abbot to "conform and adapt" himself to the individuals entrusted to his care rather than to have them conform to him. Clearly the abbot plays the key role within the economy of discretion.

One more word must be added to this semantic field—the adverb *rationabiliter,* meaning "reasonably," which appears three times joined to humility (*rationabiliter cum humilitate*). As Abba Moses says, "True discretion is not obtained except by true humility." Indeed, it is so important to Cassian that he calls humility "the mother of all virtue."

# Humility as the Mother of Virtue

In Cassian's Conference 19, Abba John contrasts the ideal of the hermit and the cenobite (one living in a community of monks). The hermit seeks "a mind bare of all earthly things and as much as human frailty permits, to unite it thus with Christ." The cenobite becomes "subject to an abba until death" to imitate the one "of whom it is said: 'He humbled himself, having become obedient until death.'" This line from the Philippians' canticle contains two key words: "humble" and "obedient."

Abba Pinufius becomes Cassian's icon of humility: This venerable old abba flees his own monastery for another; unknown there, he becomes a lowly novice carrying out "the tasks that were difficult and demeaning for the others and that disgusted everyone." For Cassian, humility becomes the radical way leading to the perfection of virtue, purity of heart, and apostolic love. Thus humility is "the mother of all the virtues."

For Cassian, discretion and humility stand in tension. Discretion demands moderation, while humility calls for the extremes found in the crucifixion. The fact that Cassian calls both of these the mother of virtue reflects these two minds.

The tension is also present in Benedict's *Rule*. His chapter on humility depends on the *Rule of the Master* (an earlier, more stringent document by an unknown author), which in turn depends on Cassian. The Master ties humility to obedience, and for him everything is about obedience. However, as you look more broadly through the *Rule*, it becomes clear that humility for Benedict is tied to service, and this is clearest in the chapter on the cellarer of the monastery. Humility allows this monk to serve the community by his obedience to the abbot and by his discretion, which allows him to do everything "with measure" and to answer the unreasonable answer "reasonably with humility."

# Love as the Mother of Virtue

Jerome, Leo the Great, Caesarius of Arles, and Gregory the Great name *caritas*, that is, love, as the mother of virtue. In the middle ages, St. Thomas Aquinas also adds his affirmation by calling *caritas* "the mother of the other virtues" as well as their "end." John Cassian, too, makes love the end or goal of humility: "when [humility] is possessed in truth, it will at once bring you a step higher to love which has no fear." For Cassian, love is not the beginning or the way, but the goal. Benedict also has love as the goal, but he also identifies it as the way of virtue, and, one might argue, even the source and mother of all the other virtues.

In the Prologue, Benedict says: "As we progress in the monastic life and in faith, our hearts will swell with the unspeakable sweetness of love, enabling us to race along the way of God's commandments." Clearly, love is not just the end but the means. For Benedict, love characterizes the basic bond of the community; therefore the abbot acts "to correct vice or preserve charity," and to preserve "peace and charity." It serves as the context of correction and also becomes the reason for obedience.

Finally, *love* is intimately bound up with service: service at table and to guests. This virtue, then, is both the goal and the way for the Christian.

The theme of love culminates in Chapter 72 on the good zeal of monks, which begins by saying that "monks should practice this zeal with the warmest love." There follow five statements defining how the monk should respect, bear with, obey, give way to, and love the other. The chapter then calls for the love of God and the love of the abbot, "with a sincere and humble love." He ends by quoting St. Cyprian: "Let them prefer absolutely nothing to Christ."

# The Source, Way, and End of Virtue

Though Benedict does not call love the mother of virtue, it clearly plays an essential and overriding role in his understanding of Christian life.

Indeed all three—discretion, humility, and love—cannot be separated in Benedict's understanding of the process of Christian maturity. All three pervade the *Rule* and work together so that nothing is preferred to Christ. Although Benedict calls discretion the mother of virtue, really all three serve as the source for the way of virtue.

> ***AUTHOR'S NOTE:*** *The ideas here have been taken from my more technical article, "The Mothers of Virtues and the* Rule *of Benedict" in the* American Benedictine Review, *60:4, December, 2009, 371-397. Those wishing more details will find them there.*

# Listening with the Ear of the Heart

*God of everlasting life, lead me in the way of good zeal—with the virtues of temperance, discretion, humility, and fervent love. Help me to be the first to show respect to another, supporting with great patience another's weakness of body or behavior, and to earnestly compete in obedience to another. Allow me not to pursue what I judge best for myself, but instead, what I judge better for someone else. May I always show pure love to all, and to you, loving fear. Let me prefer nothing whatever to Christ, and may he bring us all together to everlasting life.*

—Prayer based on Chapter 72 of the *Rule* of St. Benedict

"IF YOU SEE A YOUNG MAN
CLIMBING UP TO HEAVEN
BY HIS OWN WILL,
CATCH HIM BY THE FOOT,
AND PULL HIM DOWN TO EARTH,
FOR IT IS NOT GOOD FOR HIM."

— *The Desert Fathers*

"LET US OPEN OUR EYES TO THE LIGHT
THAT COMES FROM GOD,
AND OUR EARS TO THE VOICE FROM HEAVEN
THAT EVERY DAY CALLS OUT THIS CHARGE:
IF YOU HEAR HIS VOICE TODAY,
DO NOT HARDEN YOUR HEARTS.
... AND WHAT DOES HE SAY?
COME AND LISTEN TO ME, SONS;
I WILL TEACH YOU THE FEAR OF THE LORD.
RUN WHILE YOU HAVE THE LIGHT OF LIFE,
THAT THE DARKNESS OF DEATH
MAY NOT OVERTAKE YOU."

— *Rule of St. Benedict, Prologue, 9-10, 12-13*

# Letting Go of What Possesses

## Freeing Yourself to Respond to God's Voice

***by Janis Dopp***

A friend once told me that she was simplifying her life by eliminating many of her group commitments and paring back in a variety of ways. When I asked her the reason for this lifestyle change, she said that she had been praying for discernment about what God wanted her to do with her life, and that when the answer came, she wanted to be ready—to have "open, empty hands" that God could fill.

I have often thought of this encounter, especially when I find myself overwhelmed with busyness and "to do" lists. More than anything else, my friend was "detaching" herself from the demands that life had so easily placed upon her—demands that were not necessarily empty or meaningless, but that were not best suited to her gifts or true identity. She was not so much detaching herself *from* them as she was detaching herself *for* something more.

## Detachment: An Active Decision

So often the word "detachment" is thought of as meaning disconnected or disengaged, and it is associated with passive people who hold themselves apart from an active, involved life. Yet, detachment is probably one of the most important first steps that we all must take in developing a focused and vital lifestyle centered on being in right relationship with God.

Detachment is an active decision to take the time to recognize and let go of those situations and entrapments that hold us back from being free to respond to the voice of God when it calls us. St. Benedict's *Rule,* while written for those committing themselves to monastic life, has proven over the centuries to be a remarkable tool for anyone who wishes to embrace a life that is defined by Christian virtues. And, it gives us a wonderful blueprint for understanding detachment as the primary foundation for developing that life.

Benedict, in his *Rule,* extends an invitation to the person who is willing to practice a life of detachment: "This message of mine is for you, then, if you are ready to give up your own will, once and for all, and armed with the strong and noble weapons of obedience to do battle for the true King, Christ the Lord." This invitation is really what we are all called to accept as Christians, no matter what our vocation in life may be. We are called to follow Christ by obediently following the will of God, and in doing so, to come to recognize and appreciate our true identities. ൈ

"IT IS EASY TO MAKE OURSELVES THE CENTER OF OUR OWN LITTLE UNIVERSE, TO LIVE OUR LIVES FOR OUR OWN SELF-AGGRANDIZEMENT, OUR OWN SELF-GRATIFICATION. 'GOOD' PEOPLE FALL INTO THIS TRAP. DO NOT BE SO SURE THAT THE TEACHING OF ST. BENEDICT ON SELF-WILL IS OUT OF DATE. EXPERIENCE SHOWS US HOW SUBTLY, VERY SUBTLY, WE CAN SEEK SELF."

— *Cardinal Basil Hume, O.S.B.*

# Giving Up Willfulness

Letting go of self-will is quite a challenge in a culture that values the fulfillment of personal desire and the ability to be in control. But Benedict knew that curbing the will is basic to developing any of the virtues. It is the second step on the ladder of humility. "The second step of humility," Benedict says, "is that a man loves not his own will nor takes pleasure in the satisfaction of his desires; rather he shall imitate by his actions that saying of the Lord: 'I have come not to do my own will, but the will of him who sent me' (John 6:38)."

In setting aside my will, I become open to a wider range of possibilities in any situation, and I examine the motives behind the feeling that something has to be a certain way. It is not that I don't care about outcomes. It is that I am open to options not my own, and I am not driven by the need to be right about the situation. Giving up willfulness is also a way of learning how to forgive, for I can be just as attached to my grudges as I can be to any opinion that I hold close to my heart.

## The Commitment of Baptism

Our baptism calls us to a self-donating life in which we, as the Body of Christ, venture out into the world and become all that we can be for others. In the Catholic tradition, we are to become the consecrated bread and wine we eat at Mass. To accept the Eucharist is one of the most radical decisions any Catholic makes. Christ allows us to consume him so that we can allow ourselves to be consumed by others. We are agreeing to let go of our own plans and remain open to the plan that God has for us. It is the most profound gesture of detachment that we can enter into.

Saint Benedict advises his monks, "No one is to pursue what he judges better for himself, but instead, what he judges better for someone else." To live that kind of a life, the life that we are called to live by virtue of our baptism, takes a daily commitment to question our motives, our agendas, our demands, and our intentions.

## Image vs. Identity

In cultivating a self-donating life, it is necessary to recognize how much we are shaped by the image we hold of ourselves and by the importance we place on that image.

I once realized that I often introduced myself to others by giving my name and my work position in one seamless phrase. As I heard myself repeating my standard introduction one day, I was struck by the awareness that my job had become a real part of my identity in my mind.

Position often exercises one of the greatest holds controlling our lives. The kind of work we do often determines what we think we have to do or what we should be expected to do. We can begin to calculate our worth on the basis of how much we earn or the kind of perks that go along with the position we hold. Our esteem in the eyes of others is often established on the information we give them about what we do rather than who we are. We build assumptions on what the future will look like because of what we think we should have coming to us in the way of benefits.

Benedict had some very definite ideas about rank and how it can affect an individual's formation. On the admission of an ordained priest to the monastery, Benedict says, "he must recognize that he will have to observe the full discipline of the rule." And again, "Whenever there is question of an appointment or of any other business in the monastery, he takes the place that corresponds to the date of his entry into the community, and not that granted him out of respect for his priesthood."

Even the abbot must guard his humility. "Let him recognize that his goal must be profit for the monks, not pre-eminence for himself," Benedict writes. Taken to heart, these guidelines can be daily reminders that we are not what we do; we bring who we are to what we do. ௐ

## The Freedom of Forgiveness

Another powerful force shaping our daily existence can be the resistance to forgive hurts that have been done to us. Daily we pray to "forgive us our trespasses as we forgive those who trespass against us."

Yet, when all is said and done, it is so easy to find ourselves fondling those grudges and cultivating resentment toward the people who have done us wrong.

Thrown into an emotional situation myself, I told the offending party, "I forgive you, but I won't forget what you have done." I was sure that it was possible to go on like that.

However, I was doing both of us a tremendous disservice. To forgive while not forgetting allowed the situation to control my life. At the slightest encouragement, I could call up the entire event and replay the tape in my mind, seething with what seemed like righteous anger. The event possessed me in the truest sense of the word.

I had forgotten Benedict's commands regarding discord between persons. He says, "harbor neither hatred, nor jealousy of anyone. … Do not love quarreling. … Pray for your enemies out of love for Christ. If you have a dispute with someone, make peace with him before the sun goes down."

## Death's Gentle Reminder

Often, the struggle to change our ways is a lifelong pursuit. We need to remember—as Benedict knew—that there is a very good reason to keep trying to let go of what is unimportant and to seek God with all our heart.

Several years ago, I watched my mother slip away into the sleep of death. I sat at her bedside and watched as all the things that had possessed her through so much of her life gave way to a very focused pattern of living and waiting. All of her worries and frustrations, all of the imperatives that had driven her throughout her life, gave way to simple needs, and an even simpler sweetness.

She had let go, and peace reigned. What was important rose to the surface. She asked me to clear off the top of her dresser and to replace all of the things that were there with pictures of my two brothers and me. When I did that, she relaxed and said, "Now it's right."

I realized that she wanted to spend her final days looking at what had always been the most meaningful part of her life—her children. There were fewer and fewer words. Silence became acceptable. Simple presence was sufficient.

This paring back to essentials as death drew near taught me a little bit more about what is essential in life. It also reminded me that Saint Benedict tells his monks, "Day by day remind yourself that you are going to die." This is not a morbid teaching. It is a gentle reminder that in the end, what is really important becomes very simple and we are called to live in that sort of simplicity every day.

## Ready with Open Hands

"That which you cannot give away, you don't possess. It possesses you." This little verse came as a surprise reminder in a fortune cookie. I realized that it is impossible to give away to another the demands that I place on myself, the control I try to exercise in any given situation, my motives or my grudges.

However, I can give away quite freely my time, talents, and treasure, my forgiveness, and my gift of self. With Saint Benedict as our guide, we can all pray that our open hands will always be ready to receive freely what God is offering, and that we, in turn, will be ready to share ourselves with others.

## Listening with the Ear of the Heart

1. *What is holding you back from being able to respond in freedom to God's will for your life? Take a look at your calendar or planner to see what you have scheduled to fill your days, and then consider what you can let go.*

2. *What does your self-image look like in your mind's eye? Make a list of the talents you have, including your relational abilities. Recognize which ones you want to develop and how they can be enhanced.*

3. *Is there anyone in your life that you need to forgive? Pray for the strength to overcome your antagonism, and work toward a real reconciliation with that individual.*

"WHOEVER WISHES
TO OFFER GOD
AN ACCEPTABLE SACRIFICE
HAS NOTHING MORE PRECIOUS
TO OFFER THAN
HIS OWN WILL."

— *John Trithemius*

"DAY BY DAY
REMIND YOURSELF
THAT YOU ARE
GOING TO DIE."

*— Rule of St. Benedict, Ch. 4:47*

# Keeping Death Before Us:
## How Daily Dying Can Help Us Live More Fully

***by Rt. Rev. Gregory Polan, O.S.B.***

Some 17 years ago, I was visiting a generous benefactor who was also a good friend. He had been diagnosed with prostate cancer, and was told he had about six months to a year's time to live. I'll never forget what he said when asked, "What are you doing with the time you have left?" He responded matter-of-factly and with a wry smile, "I'm preparing for my final exam." (As I write this text, I am preparing to speak at this same man's funeral—17 years later!)

Bob could only have answered my question with such a prompt and sure response if he had lived his life up to that point with a steady view to eternity; and he most surely had. I believe that from a much earlier time, he had been "preparing for his final exam" with a life of generosity, compassion, humility, trust, and joy.

On June 10, 2002, a gunman entered our monastery in Missouri and with a rifle killed two of our monks and seriously wounded two others; then, sitting in the last pew of our abbey basilica, he took his own life. At a meeting with the press on the morning after the shootings, one journalist asked me, "Aren't you bewildered that someone would enter your monastery and then proceed to kill two monks?"

Immediately my response was, "Yes, dreadfully shocked and deeply saddened, but you know, we monks come to the monastery to die!" The five journalists and I sat there stunned by what had just been said; a long silence followed. That statement kept me pondering until I had a response that made sense to me. In the end the answer was the paschal mystery, which lies at the heart of Benedictine spirituality. By paschal mystery we mean the life, suffering, death, and resurrection of Jesus, which is to be imitated by those who follow his way.

In the *Rule* of Saint Benedict we read, "Day by day remind yourself that you are going to die." This single verse offers spiritual wisdom about bodily death. Yet, when you read through the *Rule,* you will also have a sense of what can be called "death to self," as part of St. Benedict's spiritual doctrine for imitating and following Jesus Christ. Daily dying to one's desires, wishes, or self-will can be a measuring rod for assessing how seriously we keep death daily before our eyes, while seeking the things that are above.

"NOW, [JESUS] COULD BOW HIS HEAD AND COMMEND HIS SPIRIT TO HIS FATHER. HIS LAST BREATH WAS LIKE AN EMBRACE, THE FIRST AND HENCEFORTH ETERNAL EMBRACE IN THE LOVE OF THE HERE-AFTER."

— *André Louf, O.C.S.O., Mercy in Weakness*

# Keeping Death Before Our Eyes

At the moment we pass from our mother's womb into the waiting world, our life moves toward death. To some, that thought may sound foreboding or morbid, yet it is a fact of life. This fact of life gives us perspective on how we choose to live (and sometimes how we choose to die), and how basic death is to the process of nature. It surrounds us each day. Light dies and gives way to darkness and sleep. Autumn shows us the process of dying and ushers in the winter when the death or deep slumber of so many things in nature reveals itself in stark landscapes.

However, we cannot forget that the darkness of night then gives way to the glories of a sunrise and fresh morning breezes. Likewise, the bitter cold and shorter days of winter pass to longer, warmer, and brighter days in spring, with signs of new life popping up everywhere. Nature teaches us that death is a passageway directing us to new life.

Still, it is difficult for many people to think about death. Only when someone close and dear to us passes from this world do we look at death more realistically. Or, only when we have had a close brush with death and been blessed to be restored to good health and well-being do we know what an oasis our life is.

But how instructive those painful experiences and reflections are for us. They remind us of our mortality; they ask us how we want to be remembered by others; and they forcefully teach us what a blessing virtue is, and what a curse our vices can become for us. Then the choice is ours: What road will we walk down with our remaining days, months, and years?

The Book of Sirach says it simply yet profoundly: "Call no one blessed before their death, for how each of us ends, is a person known" (Sirach 11:28).

## Wisdom as a Guide

What sobering reflection on death can teach us is not mere facts relating to life, but acquiring wisdom as one's guide. The Scriptures tell us how blessed our earthly life can be when we find the spiritual wisdom that gives direction to all we say and do.

This is beautifully displayed in the Book of Proverbs. At the beginning of Proverbs, wisdom is described as a lovely and appealing young woman whom any man should desire to have as a friend and a wife. Lady Wisdom says, "Those who love me I also love, and those who seek me find me .... For the one who finds me finds life, and wins favor from the Lord" (Proverbs 8:17, 35; see also Proverbs 2:1-22; 2:13-18; 9:1-12).

Then the Book of Proverbs ends with a symbolic poem about wisdom, describing the blessings that come to the man who has married Lady Wisdom (Proverbs 31:10-31). She does all things well, brings blessings to her husband and family, and serves everyone generously and faithfully.

The point is, befriend wisdom and you will not fear future days; have wisdom as your life's companion and the pathway through life and toward death will be touched with blessing after blessing. Cardinal Joseph Bernadin wrote of how he "befriended death" and how it gave purpose and meaning to his final months of life.

There is no one who has shown us this better than Jesus Christ, the wisdom of God. His words and deeds were a message of life and hope to those who first heard them and to those who hear them today. He approached his own ignominious death with the truth that sets a person free, and without fear of what lies ahead, trusting in the goodness of God.

## Death to Self on Life's Journey

Throughout our lives, every one of us faces the call at numerous times to "let go" of our plans, our hopes, our wishes, and our will. These entail a death to self which enables us to let go of what we had hoped for so that something else (and not always something material!) may take its place.

This is eloquently expressed in Chapter 72 of the *Rule:* "[The monks] should each try to be the first to show respect to the other, supporting with the greatest patience one another's weaknesses of body or behavior, and earnestly competing in obedience to one another. No one is to pursue what he judges better for himself, but instead, what he judges better for someone else …. Let them prefer nothing whatever to Christ, and may he bring us all together to everlasting life."

These are words that translate into daily life for every one of us, monk or not. How often should we bite our tongue rather than show annoyance with another over something of little concern? How often does patience invite us to overlook the idiosyncrasies of someone at work to keep peace in the office? How often do I have to jettison my plan for a project in a church group because another's is better—or, another's is equally as good?

Willingness to act in these ways is death to self, which then brings life, peace, and well-being—to others, and hopefully to us.

There are numerous instances in the New Testament in which the authors tell us how to live this life of virtue. If we look at any of those passages, they involve a death to self so that both we and others may experience blessing.

St. Paul writes, "As God's chosen ones, holy and beloved, clothe yourselves with compassion, kindness, humility, meekness, and patience. Bear with one another and, if anyone has a complaint against another, forgive each other; just as the Lord has forgiven you, so you also must forgive. Above all, clothe yourselves with love, which binds everything together in perfect harmony" (Colossians 3:12-14).

Who of us would not wish to be truly compassionate? Yet acting with compassion always involves forgetting about ourselves and allowing another's need to take priority over ours. Incorporating such virtues into our lives brings us blessing and deep peace of heart. There is little that brings more joy to the hearts of Christians than knowing that our lives serve others. This is the kind of death to self that Jesus exemplifies so well in the gospel: bringing hope and healing, joy and happiness to others, and consequently to ourselves.

And when we see the end of life approaching, we can remember with confidence the words of Jesus at the judgment scene in St. Matthew's gospel, "Well done, good and faithful servant; enter the joy of your Master" (Matthew 25:21).

## New Life Through Death

The single goal in life for the Christian is to become like Christ. Our experiences of death to self and of bodily death find special meaning in a passage from St. Paul's Second Letter to the Corinthians. There St. Paul writes, "All of us, gazing with unveiled face on the glory of the Lord, are being transformed into the same image from glory to glory, as from the Lord who is the Spirit" (2 Corinthians 3:18).

When he writes of "glory," St. Paul refers to the paschal mystery of Jesus into which we are all incorporated—that is how our own life, suffering, and death are now sharing in the resurrection of Jesus. But for St. Paul, our glory includes not only the promise of resurrection, but all the experiences of our life that are united to Jesus' own life, suffering, and death.

There is a little "sacrament" in nature that reminds us that our death to self is beautiful in the eyes of God. In the autumn of the year, the leaves that are turning brilliant yellow, bright orange, and deep red are actually in the process of dying. Their colors are deepest, brightest, and most brilliant as they are "in the process" of their death.

That is also true for us. Our lives mirror the beauty of God's plan for us as we die to self, and as we prepare to enter the eternal life for which we were created.

The whole process is the *paschal mystery*—new life through death!

## Listening with the Ear of the Heart

1. *What has been the spiritual impact that the experience of the death of someone close to you has had on your life?*

2. *What are "healthy" ways of keeping death before your eyes, so as to have a positive effect on your own spiritual growth?*

3. *How are you challenged daily to practice death to self?*

"GOD, CREATOR AND REDEEMER,
BY YOUR POWER CHRIST
CONQUERED DEATH
AND RETURNED TO YOU IN GLORY.
MAY ALL YOUR PEOPLE WHO HAVE
GONE BEFORE US IN FAITH
SHARE HIS VICTORY AND ENJOY
THE VISION OF YOUR GLORY FOREVER,
WHERE CHRIST LIVES AND REIGNS
WITH YOU AND THE HOLY SPIRIT,
ONE GOD, FOREVER AND EVER. AMEN."

*— Oration from the Common
of the Faithful Departed
in the Liturgy of the Hours*

# About the Authors

**Fr. Meinrad Brune, O.S.B.,** has been a monk of Saint Meinrad Archabbey in St. Meinrad, Indiana, since 1956, and for the last 15 years has been the oblate director. He has served his community as assistant novice-junior master, as a teacher both in the former high school and college, as pastor of two parishes staffed by the monks of the monastery, and as alumni director of the schools.

**Fr. Michael Casey, O.C.S.O.,** has been a Cistercian monk of Tarrawarra Abbey, Australia, since 1960. He has written several books and many articles, and has given retreats and seminars on aspects of monastic spirituality in many countries. His podcasts on the *Rule* of St. Benedict can be downloaded at *www.cistercian.org.au*

**Sr. Joan Chittister, O.S.B.,** is a Benedictine sister and former prioress at Mount Saint Benedict Monastery in Erie, Pennsylvania. An internationally known author and lecturer, she is executive director of Benetvision, a resource and research center for contemporary spirituality. A past president of the Leadership Conference of Women Religious, she has written more than 40 books.

**Janis Dopp** is a wife and mother who ministers as director of religious education at St. Charles Borromeo Catholic Church in Bloomington, Indiana. She is also a Benedictine oblate of Saint Meinrad Archabbey.

**Rt. Rev. Justin DuVall, O.S.B.,** is Archabbot of Saint Meinrad Archabbey. A native of Toledo, Ohio, he professed monastic vows in 1974, was ordained priest in 1978, and was elected archabbot in 2004. He has also worked in the Archabbey Library, and has served as prior of the monastery and provost and vice-rector of the School of Theology. He currently serves on the board of the Alliance for International Monasticism, and is a member of the Abbot President's Council for the Swiss-American Congregation, of which Saint Meinrad is a member.

**Fr. Harry Hagan, O.S.B.,** professed vows as a monk of Saint Meinrad Archabbey in 1972 and was ordained a priest in 1986. He has a doctorate in Scripture and teaches Old Testament in the Seminary and School of Theology, where he also served as provost-vice rector from 1986 to 1996. He is currently the director of cultural formation in the seminary, and he served the monastery as novice-junior master from 1996 to 2008. He also is a spiritual director, leads retreats, and has authored a number of articles. A man with many interests, he enjoys writing and translating hymns, growing tomatoes and orchids, and painting, among other things.

**Fr. Dwight Longenecker** is an oblate of Belmont Abbey in North Carolina. He is the author of *Listen My Son: St. Benedict for Fathers* and *St. Benedict and St. Thérèse: The Little Rule and the Little Way*. He serves as pastor of Our Lady of the Rosary Church and St. Joseph's Catholic School in Greenville, South Carolina. Connect to his website and blog at: *www.dwightlongenecker.com*

**Br. Matthew Mattingly, O.S.B.,** is a monk of Saint Meinrad Archabbey and holds a master's degree in Catholic Life and Thought. He has published articles in *The American Benedictine Review* and *Christian Reflection*, and has led retreats on a variety of monastic-related topics.

**Kathleen Norris**, an oblate of Assumption Abbey in North Dakota, is a best-selling author, poet, and speaker. Her books include

*Dakota: A Spiritual Geography, The Cloister Walk, Amazing Grace: A Vocabulary of Faith*, and *Acedia & Me: A Marriage, Monks, and a Writer's Life.*

**Rt. Rev. Gregory J. Polan, O.S.B.**, is the abbot of Conception Abbey in Missouri, and the chancellor of Conception Seminary College, where he teaches courses in Scripture and biblical languages.

**Fr. Christian Raab, O.S.B.**, is a monk of Saint Meinrad Archabbey, and the author of several publications on prayer and spirituality. He is currently pursuing an advanced degree in theology at the Catholic University of America in Washington, D.C.

**Fr. Joel Rippinger, O.S.B.**, has been a monk of Marmion Abbey, Aurora, Illinois, since 1968. He has served his community as novice master and instructor in its college preparatory school, as well as oblate director and archivist. He has written widely on topics of Benedictine history and spirituality, and has given retreats and served as a spiritual director.

**Sr. Laura Swan, O.S.B.,** is a member of St. Placid Priory in Lacey, Washington. A spiritual director and workshop leader in spirituality, she is the author of *The Forgotten Desert Mothers, Engaging Benedict* and *The Benedictine Tradition.*

**Rev. Dr. Jane Tomaine** is an Episcopal priest and retreat leader from New Jersey. A former manager at AT&T, she is the author of *St. Benedict's Toolbox: The Nuts and Bolts of Everyday Benedictine Living*, an introduction and practical guide to the Benedictine way of living.

**Br. Francis de Sales Wagner, O.S.B.**, is a monk of Saint Meinrad Archabbey. A former newspaper editor and reporter in Ohio, he is an editor and writer for Path of Life Publications at the Abbey Press, and studies in the School of Theology. He is also a retreat director and serves as a conference presenter for the Benedictine oblate program. He is the author of several pastoral care publications and spirituality articles, and is the editor of the recent book *Thirsting for God: Prayers from a Monastery*. Visit his personal blog at: *www.pathoflifeblog.blogspot.com*

**Sr. Macrina Wiederkehr, O.S.B.**, a monastic of St. Scholastica Monastery in Fort Smith, Arkansas, is a popular author and retreat guide in the areas of *lectio divina* and contemplative spirituality. Her latest book is *Seven Sacred Pauses: Living Mindfully through the Hours of the Day*. Visit her personal blog at: *www.macrina-underthesycamoretree.blogspot.com*

# Further Reading

*A Blessed Life: Benedictine Guidelines for Those Who Long for Good Days*, by Wil Derkse. Liturgical Press, Collegeville, MN, 2009.

*A Good Life: Benedict's Guide to Everyday Joy*, by Robert Benson. Paraclete Press, Brewster, MA, 2004.

*A Sacred Voice is Calling: Personal Vocation and Social Conscience*, by John Neafsey. Orbis Books, New York, 2006.

*Benedict's Way: An Ancient Monk's Insights for a Balanced Life*, by Lonni Collins Pratt and Fr. Daniel Homan, O.S.B. Loyola Press, Chicago, 2000.

*Bread in the Wilderness*, by Thomas Merton. New Directions Publishing, New York, 1997.

*Christ, the Life of the Soul: Spiritual Conferences*, by Blessed Columba Marmion, trans. Alan Bancroft. Zaccheus Press, Bethesda, MD, 2005.

*Engaging Benedict: What the Rule Can Teach Us Today*, by Laura Swan. Ave Maria Press, Notre Dame, IN, 2005.

*Essential Monastic Wisdom: Writings on the Contemplative Life*, by Hugh Feiss, O.S.B. Harper, San Francisco, 1999.

*Finding Sanctuary: Monastic Steps for Everyday Life*, by Abbot Christopher Jamison. Liturgical Press, Collegeville, MN, 2006.

*Friend of the Soul: A Benedictine Spirituality of Work*, by Norvene Vest. Cowley Publications, Cambridge, MA, 1997.

*Humility Matters for Practicing the Spiritual Life*, by Mary Margaret Funk, O.S.B. Continuum, New York, 2005.

*Listen My Son: St. Benedict for Fathers*, by Dwight Longenecker. Morehouse Publishing, Harrisburg, PA, 2000.

*Listen with Your Heart*, by M. Basil Pennington, O.C.S.O. Paraclete Press, Brewster, MA, 2007.

*Lost in Wonder: Rediscovering the Spiritual Art of Attentiveness*, by Esther De Waal. Liturgical Press, MN, 2003.

*No Moment too Small: Rhythms of Silence, Prayer, and Holy Reading*, by Norvene Vest. Cowley Publications, Cambridge, MA, 1994.

*Notes from a Monastery: The Sacred Way Every Day* (12-page, four-color booklets on aspects of Benedict's *Rule*), by various authors. Abbey Press—Path of Life Publications, St. Meinrad, IN. Available at: *www.pathoflifebooks.com*

Order of Saint Benedict website: *www.osb.org*

*Perspectives on the Rule of St. Benedict*, by Aquinata Böckmann. Liturgical Press, Collegeville, MN, 2005.

*Prayer and Community: The Benedictine Tradition*, by Columba Stewart, O.S.B. Orbis, Maryknoll, NY, 2000.

*Praying the Bible: An Introduction to Lectio Divina*, by Mariano Magrassi, O.S.B. Liturgical Press, Collegeville, MN, 1998.

*Praying with Benedict: Prayer in the Rule of St. Benedict*, by Korneel Vermeiren, trans. by Richard Yeo. Cistercian Publications, Kalamazoo, MI, 1999.

*Praying with the Benedictines: A Window on the Cloister*, by Fr. Guerric DeBona, O.S.B. Paulist Press, New York, 2007.

*Reflections on the Holy Rule*, by Walter Sullivan, O.S.B. Abbey Press, St. Meinrad, IN, 1974.

*Sacred Reading: The Ancient Art of Lectio Divina*, by Michael Casey, O.C.S.O. Liguori/Triumph, MO, 1996.

*St. Benedict's Toolbox: The Nuts and Bolts of Everyday Benedictine Living*, by Jane Tomaine. Morehouse Publishing, Harrisburg, PA, 2005.

*Searching for God*, by Cardinal Basil Hume, O.S.B. Saint Bede's Publications, Petersham, MA, 1977.

*Seeking God: The Way of St. Benedict*, by Esther de Waal. Liturgical Press, Collegeville, MN, 2001.

*Silence: The Meaning of Silence in the Rule of St. Benedict*, by Ambrose Wathen, O.S.B. Cistercian Publications, Washington, 1973.

*Strangers to the City: Reflections on the Beliefs and Values of the Rule of Saint Benedict*, by Michael Casey. Paraclete Press, Brewster, MA, 2005.

*The Circle of Life: Heart's Journey through the Seasons*, by Joyce Rupp and Macrina Wiederkehr. Sorin Books, Notre Dame, IN, 2005.

*The Forgotten Desert Mothers: Sayings, Lives, and Stories of Early Christian Women*, by Laura Swan, O.S.B. Paulist Press, Mahwah, NJ, 2001.

*The Intentional Life: The Making of a Spiritual Vocation*, by Cardinal Basil Hume, O.S.B. Paraclete Press, Brewster, MA, 2003.

*The Path of Life*, by Cyprian Smith. Ampleforth Abbey Press, 1995.

*The Rule of St. Benedict* (in Latin and English with notes), ed. by Timothy Fry, O.S.B. Liturgical Press, Collegeville, MN, 1981.

*The Rule of Benedict: A Spirituality for the 21st Century*, by Joan Chittister. Crossroad, Chestnut Ridge, NY, 2010 (Revised Edition).

*The Sayings of the Desert Fathers*, by Benedicta Ward. Cistercian Publications, Kalamazoo, MI, 1975.

*The View from a Monastery*, by Br. Benet Tvedten. Riverhead Books, New York, 1999.

*Tools Matter for Practicing the Spiritual Life*, by Mary Margaret Funk, O.S.B. Continuum, New York, 2001.

*Twelve Steps to Inner Freedom: Humility Revisited*, by Joan D. Chittister, O.S.B. Benetvision, Erie, PA, 2003.

*Wisdom Distilled from the Daily: Living the Rule of St. Benedict Today*, by Joan Chittister, O.S.B. HarperCollins, San Francisco, 1990.

*Work and Prayer: The Rule of St. Benedict for Lay People*, by Columba Cary-Elwes, O.S.B., and Catherine Wybourne, O.S.B. Burns & Oates, London, 1994.